T0380420

Straddling the
RAZOR WIRE

Growing up in two opposing cultures: learning to straddle the electrified razor wire of racism and other isms

Elizabeth Wiley MA JD, Pomo Elder

Order this book online at www.trafford.com
or email orders@trafford.com

Most Trafford titles are also available at major online book retailers.

 www.trafford.com

North America & international
toll-free: 844 688 6899 (USA & Canada)
fax: 812 355 4082

Our mission is to efficiently provide the world's finest, most comprehensive book publishing service, enabling every author to experience success. To find out how to publish your book, your way, and have it available worldwide, visit us online at www.trafford.com

Because of the dynamic nature of the Internet, any web addresses or links contained in this book may have changed since publication and may no longer be valid. The views expressed in this work are solely those of the author and do not necessarily reflect the views of the publisher, and the publisher hereby disclaims any responsibility for them.

ISBN: 978-1-6987-1166-9 (sc)
978-1-6987-1165-2 (e)

Library of Congress Control Number: 2022918554

Print information available on the last page.

Trafford rev.   10/11/2022

Straddling the RAZOR WIRE

Growing up in two opposing cultures: learning to straddle the electrified razor wire of racism and other isms

Dr. Bob, a friend when I worked at the ER, used to say how are your Selves today, and I started a book called Selves, about going from Cotillion in the morning in Pasadena, to the Rez, seven hundred miles north, where there were not even street signs in the afternoon. Instead of a house with a name, EISINGWOLD, we lived in the silver trailer by the creek. My parents sold the cool San Francisco house on Geneva Street and bought a new, long Lucy and Desi long silver Gulfstream to live in while my Dad built our new ranch house on the Rez. He had to put in wood terracing and buy dirt and manure to fill. it, the Rez was on steep, rocky ground, no other way to farm. He put in his own wells, and water systems.

Going to Native American sovereign reserves for research on ancient legal methodology…. in my old VW or a rented off road vehicle....as far as possible to drive, then walk with a teen or ten to translate, wayyyyy into the wilderness to talk to ancient Natives.

I then was working with gangs, etc, and started to call the book, Straddling the Barbed Wire, and then one day during a really heavy racial tension project decided it was more like straddling electrified razor wire to be multi racial………multi-cultural, multi-modality educated, seeing men AND women, NOT fights, seeing FAMILIES, not generational disputes. Seeing starvation, war, genocide, rather than what we, as humans could do on this earth each day, to help others, to maintain and restore nature, to create a better world for the next seven generations and pass that duty on.

Ps, I did know, perfectly well, that he was being mean and nasty due to my complex reality world.

Dedications

Dedications are hard: I do not want to leave anyone out, yet it would BE a book to include them all.

My sons. Tim and Dean. Without you two, none of it makes sense. Raising you with hope, and fun then moving on. Leaving you to your own lives, a new career teaching parents to cherish each moment in gratitude to our Creator who trusted you two to me, and when to let go, just the right amount at the right moments. Hard job.

Thank you for the three days in August to get me my Mom and sons all three together picture for the first time in 18 years!

Thank you to my family, the ancestors, the newest of little babies, all giving us hope and joy, the lessons of our traditions and past to grow on. Thank all of us for being people who love and let each other be, just as we are. It's a blessing not many get in life. Thank you for the visit when I came up last year, thank you for the daily media sharing of our lives. Thank you for being safe and cared for when you ask to handle your issues yourselves. God bless.

Thank you to Chris Thomas, Number 1 Realtor. Someone who believed in the 48 acre projects before even suggesting our teams be asked to put the first pilot together. RIP, friends since elementary school. The one who thought up Tuesday Night Hamburgers at Burger Continental to keep old Muir Alumni seeing each other even if we moved away for years, always welcome on a Tuesday night. Thank you for your work on the salvaging of the Statue of Liberty, and all those years helping at the Rose Parade............and so many other charities. Thank you for bringing seniors and fifty pound bags of carrots to the horses for years in the equine therapy programs. God bless, RIP. We think of you often, on that highway in the wind, in the surf of Malibu. You, and the "guys". as one by one, you gave up the big Harleys and surf days. Getting us all to volunteer for MS programs by helping us understand this horrible disease when it struck you. Thank you for driving me to Malibu when I was so disabled, sharing the dolphins, the sharks, and just the beauty as I healed. Thank you for all the hours spent sharing the horses with seniors and kids that healed each other. Thank you for Chuck and Joyce, for Norm and Jeanette. God bless.

Thank you Patricia McClaughlin, for speaking up for what is right, and standing beside the 48 Acres project with your time, expertise and skills even while in intensive care after spinal cancer surgeries. When anyone tells me their excuses for why they "can not" help others, or even themselves, I think of you and tell them. If you could, even after being assaulted by a student, in intensive care for a possibly lethal cancer surgery, but still be helping the high risk kids and veterans, they surely can find a moment to think of personal or public responsibility in their own selfish days and free time. How can this world thank you for your work becoming a "white Apache" developing bi-cultured schools long before it was accepted, let alone trendy? Thank you for getting out of surgery on your arm and getting on a bus to Selma to walk the bridge and bridge the gap of racism in America with a cast on your arm, and needing care yourself. Thank you for your years of work in S. Central Los Angeles and the San Gabriel bilingual, bicultural areas as a special education teacher and program designer for our clients education programs as a volunteer, working with interning teachers and therapists. Thank you, again just after surgery, in a wheelchair for paying for and going with young women veterans to congress to testify as they were invited about special need helps for women veterans. I might mention ladies, your programs never repaid Patricia.

Thank you to the horses, and to all who have helped with the equine therapy programs over all these years. Thank you to the dogs, goats, bunnies, ducks, cats, birds and even cow that have enhanced our programs. Thank you to the track vets who volunteered their time because they loved what we were doing so much they shared it with their multi-millionaire clients who donated medical care and offers of their influence as needed to make sure the horses who helped save and heal so many got perfect care. More than the stakes races, Triple Crown wins, and billions of dollars of ranches, and corporations, your care for our programs and our horses are trophies for your legacies.

Thank you to the probation officers, pastors, chaplains. and therapists who have brought their clients and teams to help build the equine therapy programs and make suggestions for the 48 Acres pilots for other modalities. Thank you to Jack and Jill charities for your belief in KIDS ANONYMOUS and. KIDS JR, we will never know how many kids and teens were helped by these programs, since they are, of course, anonymous. Every youth and child in those programs has gone on to share more positive life experience and help others which multiplies the help your grant helped us to give.

Thank you to Dr. David Hall, MD PhD for allowing me on his Board for freeworldu.org.

To be part of the team that developed not just the first Digital online school, from pre-K to College Prep, but to see how he and his team created the stack system to back it up and offer it to global schools, by phone if need be. To see how his medical exam prep class had led, globally to requests for similar prep classes for other professional exams, and to the final requests for an online school. Thank you for allowing our students to pilot how it worked miracles, especially for "failing" kids.

Thank you to all the women in Junior League, and other women's charitable associations for teaching me to look around, to care, to get others involved. Thank you for the fun of being one of the community volunteers who took the big Dinosaurs around to classrooms to teach everyone how to brush and floss their teeth. To be part of the fundraising global teams to take volunteers to children all around the world with their own versions of those Dinosaurs.

Thank you for the Mom of a friend who took this program to countries all around the world that just could not understand volunteering. "Work for free", you must be crazy. But she kept showing them until they realized what those Dinosaurs meant, she talked the company that makes the heads into donating them, she talked the parents into donating material for the bodies and parents that sewed to donate time and expertise to make their own Dinosaurs to teach dental health, and more than that, that volunteering is a service to the children and state.

Thank to you to all the dentists and staff that donated time and equipment into those global dental projects to save teeth for children and even their parents. Thank you for teaching us to teach others that with daily care, semi annual cleanings and check ups to find and fix dental problems, that most of us can keep the teeth we have as teens until we are a hundred years old with a minimum of loss, and to be careful in those check ups for dentists to find genetic bone or tooth problems, gum and jaw problems and keep their damage to a minimum.

Thank you to the All Saints Church, Pasadena groups that invited me to be part of "Sundaes on Saturdays" programs to visit the big teen and youth homeless centers around Los Angeles, taking big tubs of ice cream, cases of whipped cream in cans, and bags and bags of candies and other toppings for the young in those center programs. Cones and little cups for the cones and sundaes. Something so many of us take so for granted, a treat with Dad at the ice cream shoppe, or family meals and barbecues, or neighborhood block parties. A midnight snack with Mom and Grandmothers at rough times. Such a treat, such a statement of care for these broken children and teens. Thank you for sharing the moment, the seed, of hope in their lives.

Thank you to the children and teens for trusting us, even for a moment, to be young and cared for, to share their fears, dreams, disappointments and hurts. Thank you to those able to step upon those stairs of care and salvage their lives. Not for us, for them.

Thank you to the young women in lockdown facilities where they waited to be 18, most of them facing life in prison for crimes they were already convicted of as adults the crimes being so heinous. As we shared pizza, and books, they shared broken dreams, and the too often truth that the boy, or man they had committed the crimes with had turned state's evidence against them, and were already tried as juveniles, and /or given immunity for their testimony against the girls they got into the criminal acts.

These boys and men, women and girls who got them involved in crime, already back on the streets. Never heard of one that even sent $10 for cigarettes or soap to the "love" of their life they talked into crimes, and then left holding the bag. Thank you to so many of those young women who made videos and attempted to help younger women stay out of those bad relationships. Thank you to those who agreed to talk to groups of young women brought in by the juvenile probation officers for talks to help them not end up as they had. Thank you to those who joined high school graduation and then college programs to become therapists and teachers in women's prisons to help first conviction prisoners who WOULD be getting out. One of the best programs was one started by a little girl writing to her Mom about missing her and hating police who had put her in prison. That women had the courage and vision to write and APOLOGIZE to her daughter for putting a man before her love for her children. She asked her to share that apology with her sister. She then started a group of women long term, or life prisoners to help others help their own children heal of the anger and bitterness towards everyone except their Mom. And how to help them face, deal with and forgive that hate and anger before it hurt their own lives.

Thank you to the lawyers, Judges, probation and parole officers over the years who saw the hope, and the need for change, not just judgmental hate for the young men and women in the juvenile lock down and foster group programs. Thank all of you and the parents who did not give up, or give in to the antics of their children, grandchildren, nieces, nephews, brothers and sisters who needed a hug and a kick in the butt to make it back on track. Parents, Grandparents, church groups, and even here and there the parent of a child killed or maimed by that prisoner in their crime days!!

Thank you to the teachers, counselors and others that helped me stay on track of my own life, my own passions and wants.

Thank to my mentors, friends, and professional associates who helped keep each other on the road that was so often heartbreaking and overwhelming.

Thank you to City of Hope, Dr. John Frank, Dr. Robert Krantz and all who prayed for my older son when he was diagnosed with a rare form of aplastic anemia at 16. Thank you for the research that saved his life. Thank you to the horses, and their owners who lent antibodies for that research. Thank you to the Parents Club Mom who met me the first night my son was admitted into isolation with little hope for cure. She was there on third relapse for her 14 year old daughter, no more research, no hope.....she told me, we are the lucky ones. We realize the short minutes we get with our children. In her honor I started to teach parents to love and care for those few precious moments. My son was cured. The kind of cancer is now preventable, and able to be cured regularly instead of the rare deadly secret it was when he was diagnosed. What if we spent even a month of war costs and lives lost to crime on more doctors, technicians and teams to find and cure the cancers, and clean up the pollution and toxic products that cause so much of that type of cancer.

Still as that Mom told me, how often do we hear parents complain and loudly wish their kids would be 18 and gone. It comes all too soon, those who had it cut short know all too well. I was one of the double lucky ones. My son is in his fifties, after a couple of relapses, cancer free. BUT we worked hard, with cancer societies and research projects to make sure every child and teen had access to care. That those that turned 18 did not have to deal with uncaring and disgusting insurance companies that cut them off. Of even help projects that promised help, then said, oops, 18 and cut them off. WE ALL need to care. WE ALL need to look around and see the billions of dollars we spend is spent to HELP those needing help, not give some politician's relative a job they are not qualified for, obviously, because they do not find the things needed and create them, just find paperwork to torment those who need help. Read my book "Reassessing and Restructuring Public Agencies" and its second. I wrote those books to facilitate newly developing nations, and old failing nations to do annual reviews and budget audits, ALL PUBLIC, to make sure we, the taxpayers get what we voted for, and pay for. A better world for ALL.

Thank you to the Jack and Jill Foundation that gave us a grant to continue research and project development FOR and WITH kids, to form KidsAnonymous and Kids Jr. We asked AA how to use Anonymous and the 12 Steps. They said just send us an email. So…..we sent it. How many youth and teens went on to spread the healing? We honestly have no records, they are anonymous programs!

Turkey Awards/ Rotten Tomato Awards

Every life has those who get turkey and/or rotten tomato awards. The ex's who felt the week before the Bar Exam, or Medical Exam was the perfect time to tell you they were needing space. I was fortunate, my ex's, especially in view of some of the public and ongoing divorces currently in the news were great guys, just signing the papers and going their way. Saying hi years later and being friends again.

The need to list turkey or rotten tomato awards is to assure the readers and my students that I had turkeys and rotten tomatoes in my life, as they have, or will, and they can be over ridden, lived through or passed by.

First, is being born bi-racial in a state where for twenty more years it was ILLEGAL to marry an animal which Native Californians were legally. I do thank the current governor for formally apologizing for the genocide of over one hundred civilized and well grounded nations, ALL part of the eight hundred plus INCA Nation which Cortez and Columbus brought newly invented guns and cannons along with diseases and enslaved or murdered as many of the Native Nations persons as possible. THAT is four centuries of toads, turkey award winners and rotten tomatoes to override, live through, and pass by.

As you will read later, rotten turkey awards for the BIA schools, and bounty hunters sent to round up the children, as they had with most of the wild animals in California, and at gunpoint, often roped and tied up, to the "Mission" schools. For those who tortured these children if they dared to speak their own native languages. These are beyond rotten tomato nominees.

Second is the corporation that mailed out ten million samples of a product they had been sued for deaths in test marketing, so KNEW it was killing, with not one single line of warning that the product could kill or maim you within 45 minutes. I had just taken a three hour exam, part of the formal California Bar Exam, passed it in 20 minutes. Ethics. The woman asked me if i was giving up so soon when I left. I said no, finished. She asked if I did not want to go over it. I told her I had, twice. I would just start second guessing myself and lose good answers. I used that product and spent eight years learning to walk and talk again well enough to hold hot horses for my younger son who was becoming a horse trainer. He had to take me to work with him because I had recovered enough to get out and get lost, and not enough to be trusted alone. BOTH of my sons, thanks to the unjust system we call Civil Justice, having seen it in depth, had decided to turn down their scholarships for colleges and hated anything to do with a society that not only allowed corporations to call people "collateral damage", which included their Mom, but to try to beat them down, or wait for them to die to keep them from getting any kind of "justice". How does one pay a Mom for losing her career, home and worst watching her sons suffer all that AND have to take her to every doctor appointment and court or law office procedure because "justice" took so many years, before our "settlement" that both were driving by then and could READ the material. Luckily for me, even upside down across a deposition conference table…..because they were trying to ask me questions about some seventeen year old, NOT me, and HER medical records.

Third is a Congress and Court system that does NOT protect victims of this type of crime. If someone put a small firecracker or even sparkler in someone's mailbox and harmed one to five people they would be hunted down and jailed, put on trial and put in prison for years, decades. But corporations put faulty vehicles, even faultier products (if they are not a food or drug they are not even overseen) in our homes and driveways and call it "acceptable loss" when those vehicles or products kill or maim. The journalists, or employees that attempt to warn us, of do investigative reports are fired and/or seem to die convenient deaths. From police (Crossing the Rubicon) to others such as Mark Twain, Hemingway, and Hunter Thompson who tried to tell us what war is "really" about, the journalists and photographers are demeaned and lose their careers. The movie Minamata gives honor to a photo journalist who dared to try and help victims of a toxic polluting dump from a corporation is nominated for many Oscars. It took two years to get the film released by the corporation that purchased distribution rights and then kept it OUT of distribution until PEOPLE raised enough awareness another corporations purchased the rights and released the film. (Latest note: Oscar and the Academy get both turkey and rotten tomatoes for kissing ass to corporations that do NOT want a movie saying stand up for photo journalists and victims of corporate mass killing and maiming and get to call it "collateral damage". The Academy did not even give the MUSIC an Oscar…..let alone that the whole movie should be given a special Academy with ALL the Oscars nominated given because it is that great of a film, writing music acting. Most important, it's about a real person, a real hero, and reality we as humans, especially Americans who are supposed to ALL have EQUAL justice and laws, not corporate mass killers just get away with everything. THAT might get citizens looking to remember how many of their family members died from one or more corporate "collateral damage" mass murders. We sure wouldn't want OSCAR to get any part of the credit for THAT.

Fourth rotten turkey award is to the Pentagon and VA for NOT taking care of those who defend us. Friends we met, and loved. Dr. Brenda Lightfoot Young, MD PhD did not want to work with the VA, or soldiers, but they begged her, when it destroyed her life, there was no help for her. No caring anyone. Just a lot of DEA and other agency persons doing their job with not one word of care or a hug for a woman destroyed by the pain and suicides of active duty and veterans until she self medicated with street drugs. A woman assaulted and raped by PTSD soldiers and veterans she should NOT have been alone with, they needed armed guards for the safety of the doctors and nurses and staff.

How come there is no beautiful, serene place for those so broken by war ??? A place where they can heal, and heal one another. No, we need to make Congress into a parliament, that instead of meeting as the Constitution directs, once each two years for a few days staying home, WITHOUT salary to make sure each of their constituents is getting all their Constitutional rights and that no state is being allowed to run over other states, is out voting themselves raises. Playing games of mean girls in costumes rather than doing the job they were elected to do, protect the Constitution and the PEOPLE that elected them. Dr. Brenda is almost eighty years old, and only now with help of friends and a few family members will dare to go to the store alone. NOT one penny of defense department money was spent to HELP her when she fell apart. WHY is there no serene caring place for her, with her beloved soldiers and veterans to help each other heal. Because for one thing, huge bases, and often new housing was "sold" at closed auctions to private companies, or developers rather than donated to veteran, and active duty healing treatment projects. Because Congress would rather play hate games and party antics than DO THE JOB THEY ARE ELECTED, and TRUSTED to perform. I voted for and campaigned for President Obama, I do not blame him for these things, I truly believe he was told STFU and do what you are told, he had kids and a wife. What other message can we take away from the old white couple that "appeared" at their first White House event except "see how easy it is to get to y'all" Whatever his reality, he was surely not supportive to veterans or even active duty needing help, or the doctors that tried to help them.

Dr. B. is not the only one, Captain, Dr. Pete Linerooth, PhD spent years in Iraq patching soldiers back together so they could be "sane" enough to go back into battle before he finally said "done" and demanded to come home to his family. The VA met him with regulations and demands to go back for more papers and licenses to treat the soldiers he had been so successful with in battle. He asked for help, and to not make him see a "therapist" (not battle trained or experienced) where he worked. They said no, see who we say. He ate his gun.

He had told the great "they" that he needed to stop "the pain". Even low level counselors know that is a plea to end life. Instead the great "they" told him to take another licensing exam and go study with people he called "the nineteen year olds" with no thought of stress except passing a test, or getting the best grade in their class by purchasing essays and tests from students who regularly sell them on line. It was said in a news article the other night that it takes as little as ten minutes for the answers to any test to be available on smart phones and watches to cheat on examinations.

And yet, Dr. B and Dr. Pete are not the only ones begging for help from someone who could and wanted to actually help them.

We send young people to help our soldiers and veterans, but when they need help, where is Congress? Where are we. WE are probably out on the picket l lines earning our own Turkey or Rotten Tomato award for not wanting veteran programs near our homes or businesses. Just send them down to the homeless shelter or nearest skid row. There was a PBS documentary in which a woman veteran was turned away from an on VA site after care home, but the middle age, got my Master's Degree woman would not let her in because she was coming out of hospital after a suicide attempt. She said a "crazy" would upset the other tenants, and she admitted most of the rooms were available to the documentary interviewers........guess only not "crazy" veterans needed a place to heal. Veterans are living in tents along the edge of huge VA facilities, but we can rest, assured no "crazies" are in the nearly empty facilities for them on the VA sites. (Note: President Trump had demanded his new VA head address these issues, and of course the media and party gossip antics found out the man's wife had used the VA car and driver to go buy lunch for the meeting and claimed she was using it for "personal" use because she stopped along the way and bought something besides just lunch. The VA head resigned.)

WE the people remind me of the words in Charles Dicken's Christmas Carol when Scrooge says. "are there no workhouses, are there no debtors prisons". We just pat our IRS statement and say, we pay for help for them all......do we bother to see if that help is being given in a professional and caring way, in a suitable place for our heroes, children, disabled and seniors? Guess most of us are in the contest for Turkey and Rotten Tomato awards ourselves.

So, thank dedications, thank you and PHHHTTT! to rotten tomatoes. It is not an easy thing to pick who to dedicate a book to.

I do want to add my doctors and lawyers who have kept me healthy and tough enough to keep standing up for good things. Like an end to war, an end to crime and corruption that often leads to the starvation and poverty.......even the ignorance.....that leads to crime. Like our taxpayer dollars being spent for what taxpayers and voters wanted them spent for, instead of whatever they end up spent for by the corrupt. My only peace is to thank God and turn the chaos over to Him, so I can live and enjoy my. own life and do what I AM able to do to help others find their own peace path.

Writing

Benjamin Franklin is alleged to have said that anyone who spells a word the same too often is not creative.

I say, Hallelujah Ben.

I find that when writing, I want to stray away from what the great "they" say is the "best" way to write. I have gotten a Masters Degree, even after Toxic Shock brain injuries and having to learn to read and write, then type again, which took years. I also had a paid editor, but did learn the MLA language and grammar needed to write my 1500 page paper on the real research I did in Racial Tension and Gang Abatement in South Central Los Angeles, Oakland, and other areas of California that were more deadly on a daily basis than any war zone around the world. The paper reduced to one tiny subject for graduation and publication was only about 100 pages, not including the footnotes and bibliography of existing research used for the project.

I also learned the APA needed for my work towards my PhD in Reassessing and Restructuring Public Agencies, started at Cal Tech as part of the perks of my job, to become a project administrator, and take my skills and passion to make legislative goals come within the budgets assigned in the most efficient, and well overseen programs possible. The need, I found in THE MANUAL OF THE UNITED STATES GOVERNMENT (2004) which is kept up to date annually, was to make sure the taxpayers were NOT being cheated out of the services they paid for, if they at some point needed those services, those services would be there, for them. Easily obtained and given with care and professional excellence. Services which had been voted for by a Congress to exist as legislated, not to fit corrupted systems that seem to come along. I even worked with a Major from the Air Force in my dissertation class to in one night do the comparison and flagging of the previous new model of APA for the other students in our program. So up to that date, around 2010, I know APA. What a waste of time and ink.

APA. This is the way to write for the self proclaimed "perfect" two to five percent of the world population that cares about grammar, or spelling to any great degree. Especially after texting has become a daily way to communicate, these stuffy ways of writing are falling away. GOOD.

That ONE percent of the top scientists and others do NOT do the APA edits, or care about them. Their handlers and managers pay APA people to do their silly grammar and punctuation use before publishing their work.

Then a "writer" wants to struggle with "THE" way to write. Instead of saying Henry walked through the door, most would be novelists, or even autobiographic accounts of part or all of the journey on this earth, the dance for a few short God seconds (His time is not the same as ours) spends hours, months, years trying to find just the most arresting way to say Henry motived his physical and neurological skills to get his feet to maneuver his DNA and cells through the door. Then of course, another ten years or more is spent trying to figure out a way to say "through the door" so it has multiple hidden meanings for those who want to waste their own lifespan trying to figure out what someone had to say, but was too stuck in "trend" to just say, "what is this crap".

I read a paper on short, short, short stories as being the favorite of people today. A collection of these short stories being preferred over some current rendition of War and Peace, or some other lengthy well written book. Chicken Soup for every kind of Soul sells more and is read more than ANY so called "best seller".

Looking at our trend to texting, and short posts on our own social media I can see this might be true.

A couple of our favorite stories are those Jesus told to crowds. Like the children's game telephone, the stories change from here to there as they are retold.

JOKES are a great place to converse and communicate. While in law school I learned the first day that the better the Judge, or lawyer, the more they love lawyer jokes. One of the horsewomen I shared a tack room with LOVED blond jokes, she posted them on the little cork posting board on the front door of our tack room for all to enjoy as they passed by, she was a strong blond woman!.

Being able to laugh at one's self, and to not get too involved in the hate and bigotry of the world is a sure step to keep your own life more peaceful and calm.

Even reality in these areas can be funny.

One of the professors, who was a lawyer and maybe a judge told us of a story he had read in the newspapers. A man and woman were having sex in a small sports car, the man's back locked up, the woman was trapped under him and the steering wheel and seats. They both shouted for help, and she was able to get a toe up and honk the horn until someone came and called the police. The police called an ambulance after the police were unable to free the couple. The fire department and paramedics were able to cover the two with fireproof blankets and cut the roof and door off the vehicle to free the woman, and then lift the man out and take him to the hospital as his back was not able to be loosened after all that time cramped in the car seat and steering wheel. As the ambulance drove away the woman was heard to be sobbing, saying what is my husband going to say about this car. The officer waiting with her for a tow truck to arrive said, "he'll be OK, and he knows it was not your fault". The woman sobbed harder and said, the car is my husband's, the guy in the ambulance is NOT my husband.

This was a lawyer or judge joke, but it was real and from a real newspaper article.

Most of us have had sex at sometime in our lives, and it is NOT the romantic, breathy experience of supermarket romance novels for bored housewives, neither is it the four days without a break of hot, steamy sex of pornography. Sometimes it is good, sometimes it is romantic, sometimes it is easier to get it over with than to argue about it, and this is for both men and women. In many a television comedy show the man is shown to be just as filled with "headaches" as the wife, and LESS likely to want sex than his wife.

The point of this is: writing is for the writer, NOT the reader, certainly not for the critics. There is an additional part to the old motto: "those who can, DO, those who can't, teach, and those who can't do either, criticize". There are many amazing people in the world that are creative, magical, charismatic and could not teach a word about how they got that way. Others both do and teach. Many are amazing teachers that put the lessons hard wired into those who will go on to be amazing at many jobs. It is up to each of us to know everyone (except critics) is important in life. When your car is broken down, or your plumbing is rapidly regurgitating its innards into our home, or the trash is piling up in your driveway and street, you do NOT want a singer or artist, or fashion designer. But, when it is your wedding day, you do not want a football player, VIP basketball star or even a Congressperson to design the dress, veil, or plan the reception. We all want a person who at least believes in marriage, if not God and religion, to marry us. We, hopefully all, want to marry someone who loves us enough to make it to the rocking chairs on the back deck, sharing the grandchildren and stories of our lives, not someone who is "in love" with out bank balance or underwear.

Critics. These are NOT as popularly believed (mostly an idea pushed by themselves) to be experts. They tell those not able to live life honestly what to like or dislike. LIVE YOUR OWN LIFE. Better to see a few dogs at the theater, or read a few bad books, than to miss something great for YOUR life because "someone" told you it was not good. Even worse to stoically eat a a horrible meal, or sit through a boring lecture because that same "someone" said it was great. Get the story The Emperors New Clothes......how naked are YOU in all that expensive clothing you wear to try and make yourself feel OK, let alone amazing and a gift from God, one of a kind.

Relationships. One group reads romantic trash, and the other watches porn and gets their sex education from the locker room guys. NO WONDER we have so few successful, loving and lasting relationships globally. Most religious people fool themselves and pretend because they do not get a divorce, they have a great relationship. Fifty five years of drinking skunk spray does not make one good cup of water.

Instead of saying I went to a bar and met a one night stand, a writer, is carefully taught by a teacher to write a flowery, and impossibly romantic rendition of that sordid evening. Instead of saying, as I walked from my car, I slipped on vomit from someone who had too much to drink. Grasping on to the doorway, I caught my coat on the splinters of the door destroyed by the drunks thrown out by the bouncers, and finally made my way to the bar, where the table was sticky, even the basket of snacks had something sticky and disgusting on it. I ate a few anyway to not seem too eager to the glorious chunk of desperate, and drunken sexuality sitting on the next stool. Reality is not so great as made up romantics, for books to entertain the lonely and bored. The only true advisors on good, if not great relationships are O L D people who have survived the bad days, enjoyed the good days, held each other up on weak days, but who cares what they think, better get relationship advice from the ten times divorced skanks and athletes who marry each other and are featured on talk shows.

Writing

Writing is for different reasons. To teach. To describe. To share. To poke the placid folks into doing something about things that need something done about.

Writing about yourself, I feel, needs to be like talking to someone, so they can know you.

In the book, and movie (narrator) Fear and Loathing in Los Vegas, Hunter Thompson uses a style of talking to you, as if you are right there as he is living his story.

Other books, by many authors utilize a style describing the scenes to you, as a story teller, and discussing the characters in third person from a narrative point of view. We all know the sentence "The night was dark and stormy"……..as a set up for a mystery. The morning crisp and sunny….as a set up for a happy story or life.

James Joyce and other writers tell us in poetic and often extreme detail where the scene is, and how the people look, or act. The quoted words of the characters help to build the image in our brain as we read. If we are talented at reading, we see what they saw, hear their words, through their heart, rather than just eyes reading.

As a young person, I read BLACK BEAUTY and learned, having teachers, from Grandmother, not just a teacher, but a Law School. and Medical School graduate and then Dean of Rochester College for Women, to Mom, 3 Masters and a Phd, also a teacher, explain, it was not about horses at all, but how PEOPLE mistreat and abuse others and the few good hearts that are kind and generous can make life worthwhile.

My Grandmother was a Dean, because her parents. insisted she was NOT going to work with sordid details, or inner physical realities of people, it was not befitting their place in society. She instead taught other women to live her dreams until she married twenty years later to another young society member who wanted a more real life. They moved to the "wild west" where eventually he tired of that life, moved to Pasadena, California to become a beat cop, and eventually a homicide detective. She raised the children, was a socialite, helped get the vote for women, volunteered at their church, and from all the thanks I received from little old people chatting while I charted them in, or they waited for friends and relative, while I was working as the ER intake person, taught just about everyone who wanted to learn, to play the piano, from classical to whatever each one wanted.

My Mom, three Masters Degrees, English, History and Psychology, and her Social Work ongoing licensing education as well as a PhD for her work and research on "battle fatigue" as an Army Red Cross Nurse at the famous Presidio, the first active duty hospital to research and try to find cures for what today is PTSD. My Mom's Great-Aunt Mable, one of a family quartet, her sisters, herself and a half -brother who were professors at both Cal Tech and Cornell traveling the world photographing and cataloguing plants of both wild, and domestic use in the world. THEY told me BLACK BEAUTY, while a great story about better treatment for animals, was in fact, a book about the. HORROR that HUMANS have inflicted on them by an arrogant, self-appointed aristocracy and the ignorant animal abusers who served them. WOW, I thought books are often a lot more than they seem. I also was taught that often the authors had to protect their lives from death by those same self-appointed people who would gladly have one of their underlings kill the authors. Gave me the incentive to re-read Shakespeare and other great authors. Even Alice's adventures, sad to dishearten drunks and addict every where was an ADULT political commentary. WHO was going to look for subversive material in the nursery room book shelves???

Today, movies often do the same. A KNIGHT's TALE, Heath. Ledger's movie, based on the work of Chaucer told us exactly and disgustingly the reality of those "monarchs" and their "elite". When the script says "they sit at banquet, while their villagers starve from taxation" ....we need to apply this thought to our own political "tea and crumpet" consumers who pose as leaders, but instead sit around like a bad "Mean Girls" group of adults dividing the people, causing hate, and not helping our world work TOGETHER to make this a better place for us all.

Joan Baez wrote one of her books in tiny short stories, Each one with a certain memory, or points to make.

It inspired me in this book to not attempt to spend forty years creating some APA or other self appointed elite grammar police way of writing. More people have read a single Snoopy cartoon or Dr. Seuss story than ANY "best" seller. Not to say every best seller was not good. We have a take one, bring one book shelf at our church. While recovering from cancer I went to pray each day on the way home from my radiation treatments and taking care of the horses, and changed books. Many of the congregation had "best seller" book club subscriptions, so the latest and greatest were there. I think Michner's Hawaii and Goldman's Boys and Girls were two of the greatest. Mandela, Tutu, Ghandi and others autobiographies not sure they were best sellers, but members read them, and shared them…………God bless.

Music

After being brain injured from a high fever disease I had amnesia. Somethings I knew, I knew my sons, but what was not sure what that meant. If I got in my car, I could drive and some things knew by having done them, going down my street, turn right to freeway......up the ramp. The first day I realized something was horribly and terrifyingly wrong was the freeway signs looked as if written in some strange language. I could not read them.

These were not the days of cell phones, or cars that can be asked to direct you home. It is not easy to try and go back the way you came, and then not recognize your house on the street. My older son saw me sitting in my car as he left for school and directed me back home. He was eleven. Corporations can not put thousands of employees out of work, but there can be NO collateral damage from ANY product. Another job the "tea and crumpet" crowd just avoid while calling each other names and telling what I call. "yes but" stories. When citizens say "people are homeless, it is getting worse, do something, these folks start to yak about. which party is to blame and then say "yes, BUT….." some scandal that is not, and probably never will be proven. Bringing up stories from decades past, never charged, never mentioned, but a political game called men and women against each other. Instead of what do we do to stop homelessness and help those already homeless.

While doing research for my PhD. (which I did not get the final paper signed off because the mentor they finally found me said it was anti-government......how could that be, the first paragraph said THREE Presidents and their agency heads had supported the project when asked, and two had even said, WE NEED THIS YESTERDAY. One informal mentor from another institute told me, don't worry, when you write the book you have in all this research, you will be the world expert on"reassessing and restructuring public agencies. The Department of Rehabilitation agreed, hired a head hunter to find me a career position, which was found, AS a leading expert in Reassessing and Restructuring Public Agencies. But they had just found out I had deadly, stage four, level four cancer due to the TSS I had had, and said my. lovely insurance company, not covered because "everyone knew, this type of cancer was expected after TSS). I begged to take the job online, with two friends who both had excellent credentials to do my in body-presence and conference work online. In 2005 this was still be piloted and systems such as Skype, text, and Zoom did not exist. So I had to give up the job. NO ONE HAD EVER BEEN FOUND TO DO THE PROJECT I HAD PROPOSED. So the work remains undone.

Back to Music

Music was a way memories began to come back. My clinical neurologist explained it was like the roadways in my brain were burned by high fevers and deadly enzymes from the staph infection flushed by my blood flow. Those roadways in my brain, between huge parking lots of stored memory and ability. One day as healing occurred and something might be the key to a particular parking lot, a wave of memories would occur. WHO KNEW, those monster interrogatories and depositions inflicted on me by that heartless corporation would actually help me. (in truth the defense lawyer, I felt, began to know how horrible it was, just a feeling, she did her job of trying to make me think I was such a poor law student and paralegal I would throw my career away because "somewhere" down the years I "might" get damages from a corporation that mailed out samples of a product it KNEW, from marketing death law suits, was killing within 45 minutes of use, without a single word. of warning).

Certainly a memory of Bob Dylan's song of the sixties "Times They Are A Changin"..Come Senators and Congressmen, please heed the call......". This is not a game, but an end to America's vision of a world of free business, NOT capitalism, which. like communism and socialism is an elite, super. rich few who make everyone else into serfs or slaves, to just die on the side of the road when no longer of use to those who use them up. ANOTHER made up thing for the stooges to fight over. Instead of resolving problems and making our world better for all and for the earth and animals.

But music more than anything, especially in recent years has brought memories, both good and bad.

Cat Stevens. Morning Has Broken

Listening to this song, I felt like crying, did cry. Long later I remembered I used to play this song on either guitar, or piano and sing it to my tiny boys, even before they were born. I began to know what being my sons was about. My clinical neurologist a great doctor from Mount

Saint Mary's, told me that from the scans and tests, and his experience his theory was that like parking lots much of my memory was not injured, but the neurotransmitters, like little roadways. between them burned and broken. As they began to heal, and as something stirred the locks on their gates. Things would come back. Later neurological tests, not available at that time showed what my neurologists called "the black holes" of my brain. Actual parts of the brain burned by the high fevers and eaten by the enzymes from the staph infection that thanks to TSS flowed freely throughout the bloodstream.

Morning has broken was also a song we sang in choir at our church. A beginning of memories of many years of good memories of my childhood and teenage years.

Old musicals. Opera. Big Band.
World War II Dance music

These were my Mom and Dad. They went to dances.

My parents danced at home.

They danced in the street if music from a store, home, or bar could be heard. Even after their divorce.

My Mom was Saks Fifth Avenue, small private salons. For her job, she had her hair cut and styled every other week. She had her nails done every week. Once my sister Eva and I were spending time with her daughter, my niece, combing hair, having a tiny girl put forty or more tiny braids in our hair, with my horse mane rubber bands when we ran out of little barrettes to hold the ends. Painting each others nails, and toe nails with glittery nail polish, all colors we had, and glueing little rhinestones and stickers made for fingernails on. We thought, poor Mom, she never experienced this type of girl day with us when we were kids. Now years later, I realize, my Mom was a serious professional, she did not marry until almost 35 year old, She had spent years getting her hair cut and styled perfectly, her nails impeccable, from a salon, for her career. Her friends were the same. She probably never missed or thought about spending an evening with little girls putting braids all over her head with horse mane braiding rubber bands. When she was hit by a blood clot after heart surgery and paralyzed, in a nursing home, my. sister and her daughter used to go and give her facials, and do her nails. A salon beautician came in to do her hair.

One time I had to go to a very serious (I guess thinking back to the outcome) neurological appointment.

The Clinical neurologist doctor assured me that this relation to music was a good sign, the lost memory was like parking lots filled with vehicles, the neurotransmitter -roadways between those roads, and parking lots filled with memory and knowledge and the part of my brain where I actually could remember and/or manage those pieces of brain that stored the memories (and education) would over time be triggered and I would have more and more brain function as time progressed. During the interrogatory and depositions portions of my trial with the corporation that had mailed me the maiming sample......a lot of memory was struck and began to bring back things. Teaching school from pre-school up helped me as well, and MUSIC brought many things back.

Fingernails and polish.

I had been teaching with a group of girls in a modeling class working on nails, and I came into a different neurology appointment with an amazing blue color on my nails, the only color one of the girls had to share with the class. The doctor was a rather dull looking woman who obviously neither had her nails done, nor played with color as a teen or college girl. She said to me, OH THAT's what this is about. She thought, having blue nails I must have given up my impassioned career with Native American juveniles and families, and my lucrative job as a Paralegal/Office Manager in the Los Angeles office of one of the most famous law firms in both America and the world doing family law to try and get a tiny disability check. MY own neurologists had already diagnosed my injuries, and the defense lawyers for the corporation that caused my illness and brain damage had also said, the injuries and brain damage are real, we just do not think our product caused them.

I just walked out on the bitch. She obviously had no concern for her patients, or women and their health. The ONLY reason I had sued for my injuries and damages was because my friends who were lawyers said I "owed it to women". As Morton Mintz would later say about "owing women" who did NOT stand up for him when he lost his job for writing the book "At Any Cost" and his journal articles about the deaths and maiming of women from a birth control device with no warning that that corporation also KNEW their product was killing, maiming and causing death and deformity of unborn fetus when it pierced their tiny bodies, but did NOT tell that to their patients.

The lawyer Tom Riley, who finally WON a case, wrote the book about "The Price of a Life" the truth about Toxic Shock. It did not do a lot for his career, while the lawyer and talk show host who made it difficult for women and families to get help got the credit for "standing up for women". BOTH products are still killing and maiming.

Little wheel, spin and spin, big wheel turn around….Buffy Saint Marie

Hearts they shrink, and pocket they swell, everybody know, nobody tell.

Buffy. Saint Marie

Back to dancing in the streets and the music my parents shared.

USO Dance music. Boogey Woogy Bugle Boy, I think because of the Army Nurse uniforms worn by at least one band on a variety show on television singing that song, it reminded me of my Mom.

Soldier Boy as well. My Mom has pictures in her Army Red Cross uniform, she was tall, and very beautiful.

My Mom had been a choir mistress at her family church while in college at UCLA. She often sang children's songs to us.

My Dad liked "Doggie in the Window" and when they both left the military, sold the big San Francisco house and moved to the Rez, he got us a beautiful Chow named KING. Someone dumped two cocker spaniels on the rez, that soon became Mom and Pop and the Little Blackies.......sadly, in ranch country, they decided to go visit the ranch next door and kill a sheep. They had to be destroyed. My Dad did not cry, he just shot them. It's the law in ranch country, either him, or a group of gun bearing strangers. My Dad did not get another dog for fifty years.

One day, some years after my Dad had passed, I was driving and the song about an old man and his dog came on the radio. I had to pull off the freeway and sob. In the song, Beau Jangles, are the words, and the dog he died, the old man cried.

My Dad had gotten a call one day from a friend who ran the only pound on that reserve. He said he felt upset, he hated to put down animals, but someone left an ugly dog there, and no one wanted it. My Dad said, I will be right there. Yep, he said, seeing a little Terrier mix of some kind, that. is a "mighty ugly dog" and took that pup home, fed him "Mighty" dog food and named him "Mighty Ugly Dog". Mighty never knew how ugly he was. Dad had him professionally groomed. He wore suits, rain coats and boots in the rain and snow. And one day, long years later. Mighty passed.

My heart was broken. My Dad and his wife Mary had two small white poodles, groomed, rhinestone collars, painted toenails, and cool clothes and bows. But I wanted Dad to have more years of what he called "an NDN and his dog". I knew he had always wanted a Pug, because he said their dark little muzzles looked to him like him with his dentures out, or before they installed his implants. That had to be the year not a single pug was available. I found ONE, $600 for a tiny pup. I thought what? Is that $100 an ounce. Then I saw a rescue ad that said mix Pug. I called. She said, just pay the spay/neuter and shots and you can have her. We set a date to pick the pup up.

The rescue called and said, we hate you to drive all this way, this is a (magic words) ugly dog! She told me the pup had been brought in because it was so ugly no one wanted it to the pound, the workers ALL loved the happy, loving little dog, but no one adopted the ugly little girl. I said, music to my ears. She told me the pound had not wanted to euthanize her so asked if she would try to find it a home. They had just about decided it was going to be a mascot at the rescue, but give one more try to find her a home and published the ad. I knew, when I saw her, this is the perfect ugly dog for Dad. She was perfect, beautiful Pug except for her face, it was some kind of wiry Terrier face with kind of a squishy nose like a Pug. She was instantly loving. as I drove her to the airport. My friend's Dad lived by the Yakima Airport and was going to meet her and take her to my Dad. The airline people, Larry's Dad and his friend, and finally DAD. Except for when he was in hospital from to time she was with him until his death. He had moved to Rez senior housing when Mary passed. The Poodles long gone, and her daughter took Dad's huge aquarium and Pug nosed black and gold fish with her, not wanting to admit they were his. She took all his furniture as well. My cousins and Uncle tried to help and got him into the senior housing with Friendly. as he had named his Ugly Pug. When he passed my cousin took her home, in our Native American tradition to never disrespect the bond of NDN and dog. Now of course he and Mighty and Friendly are together across that Rainbow Bridge. And that song still makes me cry!

Love Songs

There are songs that remind me of people, of the best times. Of the hard times.

Fifties

The songs of the fifties remind me of growing up on the Rez. The love songs were those played on radios, mostly on car, or truck radios by my cousins. In those days kids, rich or poor, no matter what culture or race, worked on farms or ranches to help earn money for the families to make it through the winter, pay for higher education and buy things they needed or wanted. Almost all of my Native cousins lived on small farms or ranches purchased by their parents on the GI Bill. Something I would not understand or realize for years was that allowed them to buy new cars, their own farms or homes, and clothing most Rez kids could not afford. A big part of that reality was that my Mom was rich, white, educated and had been both a Social Worker and Army Red Cross nurse, and a teacher for the Roosevelt programs. SHE not only insisted each one get the benefits and education they were owed, but also knew how to get the paperwork completed to get those rights for them.

This actually created a strange situation, most locations Rez kids were bullied, not wanted around, in California not allowed to go to school, but many women, had, like my Grandmother married a California-Spanish man, left generations down from mission soldiers, or workers. The school district thought they were Mexican labor kids and let them attend. Once they thought, "that Mexican housecleaner" was the Mom, or that. "Mexican field worker" the Dad, they never questioned the other kids. My Dad and his only whole blood Rez brother both went to the school as Mexicans. Not wanted, but legally allowed. Both of them did well enough to enlist in the Army and graduate from the GI Bill provided college afterwards.

Most o f my cousins and the older brothers had been through high school, military and out on their own by the time my Dad's brother was born, and then my Dad. Enough of the families in about 50 Rancheria Rez locations had worked in the Levi Strauss Company since it opened to sell jeans, overalls (overhauls as the locals called them) and down the decades the jackets and shirts, bandanas to create a Northern California Native dress tradition of jeans, usually by the fifties black jeans, blue jackets, and tee shirts with military boots brought home after whatever war someone had been drafted into. Cowboy boots, the fancier the better. Used to men me wonder…..no one had horses at that time, just face cars and motorcycles. Almost every male cousin or Uncle I had owned and wore expensive black leather biker jackets except at work, since many of them worked in offices and banks thanks to my Mom's pushing.

The old fifties songs remind me of the girls I met at camp. Again, radio and small single record players owned and sneaked into the camp by girls that today I realize were there from foster care, or juvenile probation. Usually kept away from the rest of the campers in their own groups except for meals, campfire and singing or performance nights. My friend Eloise (later called herself Bobbi, I called myself Lesli after my Dad's middle name) and I got sent to camp for most of the summer while our Moms worked and it was not time to get sent to our Dads for their part of the summer child duty. The back and forth marathon of divorced kids as it was called. Not likely to help make a child feel loved, especially when one end of the marathon was all whites who hated brown people, and the other end brown people who hated even half white people, no matter how they all loved my Mom and her parents.

After a couple of weeks at camp, Eloise and I got put in with those foster girls because we tended to get the other girls in trouble. We used to leave before breakfast and walk to the stables. a mile or so across the mountain and help feed, groom and saddle the horses and go out on all the trail rides to help anyone who needed help. When we got back, we got to wash the pans and help clean the kitchen for our misbehavior. We loved cleaning what I called the Big Kitchen, huge pans and pots, and cookie sheets. Huge sinks. SPOONS the size of big mixing bowls. AND we got to eat what the cooks created for themselves after the kitchen and dining room were cleaned.

Both Eloise and I were essentially innocent little girls, caught in the reality of divorced parents working and taking their share of making sure we went to ONE school, and spent as much time as possible with both extended family members and sent to camp to be safe during part of the year when no one was able to care for us. My brother and sister were also at camp most of summer before going to Dad's.

We, for good or bad, were put into cabins and tents with girls who had survived the worst of group homes, juvenile detention centers. Often looked 18, but were 12 to 16.

I always remember one girl, Sue E. not even 16, had a checkered and heartbreaking sex life, and home life which had put her into the detention center. In later life, I would remember that both Eloise and I helped them be teen girls, laughing, fun, and forgetting for a moment trying to be "adults". Smoking, drinking, sex talk, I saw not one of them got a letter from any of the boys, or men who regularly took advantage of them.

And they taught us how to NOT fall in love with lots of talk, useless men as we listened to the realities of their lives for anyone, but especially for girls so young. I had no idea how learning to love them would make such a difference my career years later. Even today in many of the worst women and girls I have worked with, I see, if I look carefully, those young and broken girls and hope someone helped them.

I also realized years later we had our parents and family on both sides to teach us to live with sense. Not boring, just not falling for every con man who passed by either. I later even realized how many of my Aunties and cousins HAD fallen for them. Of course a big part of Rez life was seeing the rich, white ranch sons treat my cousins in a way I would not know for years was called racist and classist. Many of my cousins had babies with hose white ranch jerks. I was a kid, no one noticed me, but I saw more than one of my lovely, graceful and smart cousins be broken by a guy she thought loved her when she told him she was pregnant. Some of the families for whatever reason wanted their Grandchild, and threatened they would take them legally until they ran smack hard up against my Mother. As usual, she had made it a point to know the Judges, Sheriff, and State family workers as well as the BIA and Congress and Senators. Native Californians were legally not even people yet, but my Mom made sure those girls kept their babies. I had no idea that had been a big part of her job for war brides, brought to America with soldiers who loved them and married them, had a child or two, but when their racist families got to them, dumped them flat. Some of THOSE grandparents for whatever reason wanted their "half-breed" grandchildren. It did not matter if those young women were French, British, Irish, or German, those families did not want their son married to "that trash".

Another curled razor edge on that electrified fence for me to to see and land on. I could. not see anything but children and wives left alone in a strange country by the "men" who loved them.

I remember one woman, my Mom was trying to help her keep her child from the grandparents and the "old" girlfriend their son had "come to. his senses" and was now going to marry. Just take the child and leave the wife he brought here with "love" alone and afraid. Her name was Sydney, she was also very beautiful. I never knew, being just a child, her background, just she was a "war bride" now unwanted by the father of her child. His family did take her to Court. She gave me an expensive and fragile gold bracelet and committed suicide over fear of losing her child and being alone, not even speaking much American.

I kept that bracelet for decades and finally sold it to help establish a program for a new era of unwanted war brides and their children. I hope in all my wok, with women and children to have Sydney's angel watching and smiling finally. God bless.

Buffy Sainte Marie, Joan Baez, Bob Dylan

The Universal Soldier, I heard Buffy (AND SHE WAS NATIVE AMERICAN and brown and looked like ME!) and some of my life began to make sense. I spent a small amount of my year on the Rez, which in reality meant visiting the Rez itself, very small, 73 craggy, rocky acres or the ranches, farms and home of relatives scattered from San Francisco north to Oregon.

A couple in Oregon, Washington, Idaho. and visiting native nations across America with my Uncles and much of my Dad's family, who were Assembly of God Preachers on Native Nations and often traveled to visit other nations or give big tent meetings.

Spending part of my year at camp while my Mom worked, and the rest of the year in Pasadena, CA going to school where all the girls were short, blond and nasty for the most part. The handful of us NOT fitting into their cliquey gossipy groups suffering until I or a few of us had a "conversation" with them on the way home from school and they stopped being so nasty. I was one of those kids that protected smaller kids, the disabled and made some stand up to bullies WITH me.

My Dad used to tell us, what people call you, who cares, but if they get close enough to hurt you, beat them so bad they will never dare to even think of you again. My sisters and I and some other minority friends all laugh as we think of our antics. Bobbi, while white, was Jewish, so one of us minorities having to stand up for our own safety and to stop bullies. We were kind enough to stand up for other kids too!

How did songs about peace, civil rights and end the bomb, end war, and end the draft lead this group of hellions into its circles? Well, part of that is Pasadena, Cal Tech and JPL which were globally integrated scientists and engineers, giving our city a new and strange way of life. We would not realize that until decades later at a reunion. Maybe 50??? Sitting at our old campus and looking around to see every race, culture, religion and men and women who had been friends at that high school BEFORE federally mandated bussing and integration began.

We were the "bad" school. Across town the campus of the school of rich and often racist kids sat. We had been to middle school with most of them and did not miss them in high school. We had our share of "mean girls" who would later be the ones we realized were cliquey and thought they were better than everyone else. Guess we all fooled them, we did not think about them at all.

I do remember one football player, came from another state and while he was breathlessly good looking, it took about a week before the girls all disliked him, and were glad he partnered up with one of the "clique" of cheer leaders. He was one of those guys who believed all the locker room bull and thought every woman or girl was just. drooling to be with him. His rude, disrespectful attitude towards women made sure we all thought he was a step away from being a serial rapist.

I also remember that cheerleader going off to "trip to Europe" one holiday or summer. She came back pale, and not so sparkly, he had, of course found someone else while she was gone. It would be years before I realized WHY she left a young girl and came back a broken woman from her trip to Europe. Abortion was still illegal in the State of California and the United States.

I did notice that other girls stopped sparkling and were expelled. I would find out, again years later, they had had a baby. I did wonder when I did find out the truth, how come the boys, the fathers, were not also expelled. I had hit another spike on that razor wire. I thought we should facilitate for things to be best for mother, father and child. Who wants to come into the world with the tag "unwanted" stapled to you.

I certainly thought we should have better sex education.

When my sons were 13 or so, and my nephews, I said, here's the deal, a girl shows up at the door and says "I'm pregnant" do not open your mouth to say "How do I know it's mine". If you are that careless and hang out with girls that might have more than one sexual partner at the same time frame, that's your problem. YOU will be a good Dad. I won't expect you to marry anyone, but no fighting. AND YOU will be a good Dad. Even today with DNA I do not want to hear that stupid "how do I know it's mine" mean statement. I think if a man can not trust a woman he has sex with, he should not have sex with her. What if its AIDS next time, or a deadly boyfriend with a gun?

I must have been convincing, most of them do not have children, the ones that do waited to make that decision and have taken care of their children, and for the most part their wives, even if divorced, remained good friends and co-parents!

The Surf Generation In California

The surfer from California spread from Hawaii where the Natives had surfed for thousands of years. The story, now seeming to prove out in DNA unless a LARGE number of west coast veterans brought wives home from WWII service in Hawaii is that a huge undersea earthquake was foreseen by island healers. (Healers are discussed in another part of this book). The tsunami from that earthquake was foreseen, so those islanders built boats and came over to the mainlands. These traditional stories seem born out in many areas by the creation of clothing and the art. One archeologists had this story in his mind so much that he made models of the island boats and actually sailed them on the Pacific currents to see if it could have happened. He did manage to make it, but the majority of opinion was that it was a fluke. He also made it back! However new studies of shipping routes from later years seemed to support that those currents do have times of the year that could have simply bobbed those little island ships to many landings along the western coasts of North and South America, and back.

Traditions tell that in their own traditions many Native West Coast people at one time did return to their islands.

AnyHOO, surfers by the fifties and the sixties were becoming more and more active on the coasts of California. The Beach Boys, Jan and Dean, and other surf bands, often just one album, or even one single record. Surf bands played at the beach parties that were legendary in the early sixties. Some areas were more Beach party movie type parties of more party than surfing, others were little driftwood fires in beach stone and sand shoved together to create fires with driftwood used to cook hot dogs and marshmallows. Most of the purchased items bought with money from everyone gathering bottles on the beach and in the parking strips along the highway up and down the coast. A lot more surfing than party at those scenes.

Gas was less than 30 cents a gallon at the expensive gas stations, bottles were taken back for five, ten and 25 cent recycling payment. We often gathered enough bottles during the day between morning surfing and evening surfing to shower at the beach. bathroom outdoor shower, put on jeans or shorts and a nice shirt and nice sandals and eat at the many expensive seafood houses along the coast. It was a great time to be a teen, even if you had NO money. Many of the surfers taught surf lessons and lent out their boards to their students after school, or on weekends to afford cheap room rentals near the beach, or lived at home if they lived near a surf beach.

I generally saw the strangeness that all the girls tried desperately to tan before putting on bikinis, so they did not blaze shockingly in the sun of the beach. YET, they did not like brown people! Orange County was one of the worst places for racism. I tended two hang out with my high school best friend, who was a surfer, and also Irish with a Mom who lived across the street from the big surfing area at Huntington Beach, so no one said much to me......but I did not have to try too hard to tan!

Beatles. And Other British Bands.

MY Ex was lead singer in a surf band at San Gabriel High School, when bands started turning to BEATLES and he grew already longish surfers hair. (it was against the rules to attend most public schools with hair that was below the ears, so most surfers had hair shaped at the bottom by a barber and long and styled in from the top so the long hair was legal, it did NOT go below their earlobes, but was long as much as they could get away with it. People often wonder about strange fashions, that is how that hairstyle got started out here in California in the mid-sixties.

People still married their high school sweethearts, and we did. Both had started college, went to the Priest for those classes, but mostly just knowing the draft was coming, he had missed it a moment because he was the only son of a Mother with cancer who was terminally ill. She died. We even had a written contract of our intentions towards our families and any kids if we had any. He had started both business and Japanese majors and minors, because he was networking to become a. business translator for a huge motor company based in Japan. I was in Administration of Justice intending on law school and helping Native Americans bridge a bicultural gap and learn to build lives that fit their own traditions and beliefs, but survive in the reality of life in the dominant money culture. To take tradition and slide it into the financially dominant culture by easing the boundaries, not erasing them. Diversity and bicultural development had not begun as of yet. Truthfully, most Native Americans were still considered forest bunnies who waited for the great "civilized" to come and 'free" them from their horrible lives of no war, no crime, no child molesting, no sex trafficking, no fights over property. Many Native Nations, such as my own from Northern California maintained even no death benefits. A parent gave their items and items included housing to the child, or nephew or niece that was taking care of them, Anything not given away was cremated with the person and discarded. By the time the Catholic Missions had put their hands around the throats of tradition, a mass of superstitions included "ghosts" which clung to all not-gifted property and it was crushed and discarded into the ocean in a few spiritual spots. The Missions had put the idea of burial on many, but the rape of children in the BIA church based schools forced many in the twenties and thirties to join small born again churches which allowed them to be "saved" and "born again" without the burden of being a "savage".

MY COUNTRY TIS OF THEY PEOPLE ARE DYING. Buffy Sainte Marie.

Another Native American song, along with Now that the Buffalos Gone that led many of us into research on our own traditions.

We realize now that we were fortunate because we belonged to large groups of teens that had already gone to very exclusive private schools, and public schools with children of world scientists working at Cal Tech, and Cal Poly Pomona, so were very diverse in our friendships.

We did not escape racism, or gender or financial bias, but going back for reunions at John Muir High School we realized we had lived in a small bubble of diversity and friendship. My friends included the bikers and the athletes, the chess club and the top students headed to Stanford, and even the guys from two huge military academies for super rich teenage boys to prep them for the Military and Air Force, Annapolis, Army and Marine officer college training programs. These young men had to learn how to behave when they were in the academies and chosen to represent their branch of service in White House and Congressional events.

I was fortunate enough to have a friend of my Mom who had been a Broadway show dancer that retired and opened a dance school. She gave free dance to girls from the local private and public schools if they came to the events to train those military academy school teens how to behave and how to dance. We learned all the different ballroom dancing specialties expected in high society, and taught them. We got to dress in ball gowns and learn, and teach those students how to behave in the highest society balls and events.

How fun, and they ALL were so good looking and athletic. We had no idea its was because of the great medical care, nutrition and expensive clothing they had. All of them had to take classes not offered to even private school teens. Swordsmanship, Fencing, marching and presenting arms for prestigious military and political events. It gave them all a kind of "pirate" smoothness and valor. Since some very wealthy world scientists lived in our area from JPL and Cal Tech, both of which supported the United Nations and its promises of diversity, these programs all were fully integrated as well. Except I began to notice. No Native Americans. I believe my little brother would have been accepted had he applied, but he was not on that route. SANTANA was more my brother than Stars and Stripes Forever. When he finally went into military it was as an engineer and electrical technician to de-fuse misfired missiles in tanks too expensive to allow to be wasted in Germany when the cold war led to the Berlin wall and it being patrolled by tanks that appeared to have uncooperative missiles.

Elton John. This Is Your Song, Tiny Dancer, Don Mclean . American Pie

People have no idea what the not war in Vietnam was, it was a police action, no threat to the United States, and not Constitutionally legal for the US to draft our citizens, kids, at that time not allowed to legally smoke a cigarette, or buy a beer, or vote to go get killed in. To come home with what now is recognized as untreated PTSD. Having studied criminal law and my Mom working with veterans since World War II, researching what was then called Battle Fatigue, today PTSD, I began to recognize how many serial killers, serial rapists, and mass shooters were in fact, untreated PTSD veterans. Many slipped notice because they got injured in bootcamps, or today before their 14 months of mandatory service to be considered veterans. In our programs we did NO paperwork, if a young person had signed the papers at the recruiting station and fell on the pen, VETERAN. We also do not believe PTSD is a mental illness, it is a sensible response to something so horrible none of us can imagine it. For some, especially those with no treatment or being labeled as mentally ill, and given medication that ruins their chance of a life after that date, without hope, turned to drugs and crime. and became monsters.

In my huge urban high school, we DID notice the large number of boys (and they were boys) drafted before graduation, and sent to boot camp, by 18 or fall, whichever came first, they were "in country" which means deployed. Then we noticed they were not coming back or if they did, they were drug addicted, or suffering from what today is known as PTSD. The no, not war, and no draft for no not wars movement began to spread into local churches and community groups of very conservative people.

I remember every time I hear someone say "defend America" meeting a friend from high school. He had returned from Vietnam and disappeared. I sat next to him on the. wall in front of his brother's clinic. His brother had managed to stay in school and was a doctor because the war ended before he would have been drafted as a doctor to serve the troops and veterans. My friend began to tell me of the trainings just sixty miles from where we sat to teach young Marines to storm out of troop beach landing boats after being offloaded from ships carrying troops. In training the Marines waded out, loaded on to the small beach landing boats and waited as the group of training boats went out a bit, then backed into the beach, flopped the unloading ramps down and the entire boat of Marines flew out, shooting as they screamed and hollered Maine learned mottos about death to all.

He said when he got to Vietnam, they unloaded off the big ships, and then the boats rushed towards the beach, ships and boats as far as the eye could see both to the right and left of the troop unloading boat he was on. He, like all the rest, loaded and readied himself and burst out in the wave of Marines up on to the beach, firing at the lines of enemy fire. He said he was well up the beach before his mind wondered, why is this beach so rocky? Then he realized, it was the bodies and helmets of the Marines jumped out for hours before their troop landing boat landed. Dead and dying boys. He managed to survive that day, and months before being injured enough to be told "man up" and go back into battle. He had not survived the feel of those "rocks" on that beach. As far as I know they still haunt him.

My Country "Tis Of Thy People
Are Dying Buffy Saint Marie

THE STAR SPANGLED BANNER

On Fourth of July 1970 our church had a huge support the veterans and deployed soldiers of the not -war event. Our church's national leadership had met and come to a conclusion that war was surely something Jesus would not have agreed with, or with a church saying God is on our side. On that evening the 5,000 seating plus church spread out on to the lawn, and downstairs to the forum where the speeches were able to be heard. Ron Kovic and some other Vietnam Veterans came to speak. A guy named Mike Lee, not his real name, everyone knew, from the emerging group of veterans who had been special ops that later became the Weather People also in the group of Vietnam Veterans Against War also spoke of the disgusting, genocidal war we had sent them to.

As our family left, we saw Ron sitting alone in the parking lot. He was in his wheelchair, waiting before getting in to his specially equipped car so he could drive it with hand controls. It was his birthday, the entire event group of possibly 10,000 people had sung happy birthday to him, yet, here he was, alone. You can see the Oliver Stone movie "Fourth of July" or read Ron's book "Born on the Fourth of July" to find out how Ron went from being one of the most well known and beloved Boy Scouts, high school wrestlers, high school baseball players, expected to be recruited at least into the minor leagues, to the guy sitting alone in a parking lot wrestling with the reality of being a paraplegic from having been shot in Vietnam and coming home to find a VA that abused the veterans. A society that spit on them and called them baby killers and forest burners (This was before the pictures of Mei Lei and the reality of Napalm and agent orange came home to America). Our Reunion group found that over 700 members of our high school in the three years we had attended were gone, their last known address: the US Military in one branch or another.

We asked if he wanted to come home with our large group of family and friends, he said yes, so someone stopped for a cake at a bakery on the way home. We all cooked dinner in our big family house, an old Victorian 1880 Craftsman my Grandfather had rescued from a tear down near 1914, and moved to the lot he had bought to set it on. The house had been on millionaire row, built for the disabled wife of someone. Every door was wider than usual to fit her old fashioned late 1880's wheelchair. It made Ronnie really happy that his chair fit through the doorways to our house, and no one had to carry him from car to house, and the bathroom was big enough for wheelchairs of the past century, perfect for his use! Over the years we met many veterans, mostly young, broken in body, mind and soul ………for what?????

Ron gave me the song "Tiny Dancer" by Elton John as well as "This is Your Song" Ron was learning to play the guitar, and in the phase of lyric writing of "Roses are Red, Violets are blue", and silly rhymes that put together meant nothing, but were funny. The boys and I used to go stay at his penthouse on the beach in the Venice area of California because he was often traveling and we loved the beach. I was renting a huge family house from my Grandmother's estate. My sons were not in school yet, and when not in school myself, I was studying Administration of Justice, towards being the first Rez woman to be admitted to LAPD Academy and later law schools, I had wanted Stanford, but they were not so keen on women, let alone Native American Rez women. Native Americans were not allowed to study arts, dance, drama, only business. I decided on Administration of Justice to go out on reserves around the country and create and implement bi-cultural administration of justice programs. Even though paying for my own education, I was shoved into what at the time were called CETA programs that were supposed to "develop" third world peoples and savages (not their word, but obvious from some of the teacher's and students attitudes). Every student does have a few free classes, so I did take some art and photography, ceramics and drama. A great thing about Pasadena City College was that often professors were one time, or just one class a quarter taught by professionals. Our Administration of Justice classes were often taught by real administrative level justice professionals.

Various family members and friends rented rooms so they could attend Pasadena City College across the street. Ron stayed at our house sometimes and when he rented a house in Venice, again the boys and I stayed there while he was traveling for Vietnam Veterans Against the War events and speaking engagements. "Pirate smile" in tiny dancer made me laugh, many people besides Ron had noted I had a "pirate smile". I liked it. It fit in with the thought of the Bob Dylan song my ex-husband had assigned to me in high school, "She Belongs To

Me". "She never stumbles, she's got no place to fall, the law can't touch her at all" words to inspire a young Native American working on salvaging Native tradition while working within dominant culture Administration of Justice boundaries to reduce the conflict between Natives and invaders. That tiny dancer also had a "pirate smile" and had been a ballet dancer.

It was around this period that I was working as a paralegal for a friend in Amnesty International. A graduate law student out of Harvard, his Quaker background had put him in a group very interested in the need to make sure law was used to protect EVERYONE from corrupt and unconstitutional actions by people more interested in their own wallet than the rights of people throughout the world. This is where I learned about what today are called "warrior lawyers". Those that actually have ethics and believe in justice for ALL.

Peter, Paul and Mary, Bob Dylan, Joan Baez and many others over those years, of civil rights demands, women's rights demands, and stand up, Constitution in hand, to say NO draft for undeclared wars, only wars in which our actual shores were in threat. President Eisenhower, in his last speech to the nation, warned us of the selfish, self serving military industrial complex building forces for taking over our country. The 1944 RAND REPORT on the feasibility of a united world without need for further wars described strategies that "might" be used to control the whole world. This was a think tank, not a government strategy plan. One of the "strategies" was to lead the two huge countries of China and Russia into war, and then drop the newly invented nuclear weapons on Moscow and Beijing. The thought being that those countries had one seat of power, while America was designed to withstand any central take over. Each State had the power and systems to stand alone, to build a new Federal center even if Washington DC went the way of the test bombings in Hiroshima. and Nagasaki. (NOTE: Americans best not let anyone take our independent State's rights and County Rights, City Rights and Individual Rights away or try to make our ONE Federal city, to guard those rights, NOT be an involved state away). The more independent and separate we remain, the less likely it is for anyone (foreign or domestic) to take over and make us all serfs or slaves in our own country).

The testing of newer and newer bombs was often done in deserts, and mountain areas, now still infected with the residual radiation and radiation poisoning. Leaving radiation to blow in the winds, creating newly polluted air, water and dirt. Currently (2022) tests shown on the news by local residents appear to prove evidence of residual radiation in soil samples, now uncovered by wind and time, blowing dust and it appears, radiation into the housing developments built years after the testing. There is conflict between private labs hired by the residents, and the administrative agencies responsible for the clean up almost 70 years ago after testing. This appears to lengthen the time thought about how long the effects of radiation can last after bombs, or other radiant material spews freed radiation and the resultant radiation poisoning effects.

No one knew, but they learned fast. Scientists led the end nuclear testing and thought of uses other than blowing us all away 70 times each. Most of us only get to die once anyway. In the movie "Harold and Maude" which did not get awards, or fame, was called a "cult film" it was pointed out that war had become obsolete at the point that WWIII would result in a 70 times death of every living thing on earth, as well as lasting 70 years at least into the future. Even those in shelters would run out of food, and water, and die. If, by some impossibility, a baby born on day one of the bombings survived in a shelter, that person would be 70 years old before ever seeing sunlight. Coming into a world barren of all except certain species of cockroaches, because, yes, the scientists tested to see if any living thing could survive. They had no idea at the time what the results of all the radiation and radiation poisoning would be in the cockroaches. What would be the generational changes??? It convinced the most insensible of people to decide nuclear war was not a win, so move on, to detent and the cold wars. (and I fell on to an especially sharp blade of that razor barbed coil fence).

The nuclear nightmare had come and was at a restless impasse. John F. Kennedy stood against the power pack his own father, old Joe, had put in place, and was being threatened for it. One thing was clear, nuclear war, in its essence is like the movie"War Games" no one will ever win. That is proven out science. The emergence of huge areas of "dead sea" from testing nuclear weapons under the ocean and the poles is evidence pure and simple of the ongoing and longstanding problems if radiation escapes and poisons our earth. A quart of this "dead sea" water can be mixed with more and more water (which obviously is what happens in ocean currents). The expected result, of the good water restoring the radiated "dead" water did not occur. The "dead" water expanded and killed the good water. Nothing could live or grow in it. I read recently that oxygen can not exist in the radiated water, making it totally dead since nothing, not even the tiniest of plankton can exist without some type of oxygen form in the water. The scientists are not saying what they are finding out about the WHY the radiation has that effect. The last seminar I saw on this subject, dirt, air, water all are being studied to find ways to end the radiation itself, and the radiation poisoning that may exist for up to 70 years. Most important are the studies of NOAA and Yale on this subject.

HAS ANYBODY SEEN, my good friend Abraham, John, Martin, Bob?.......(Hollerd and Gernhardt, 1966) Originally, notes Wikipedia, written for background in a Snoopy Red Baron project! (rewritten by DION in1968 to include Rev Martin Luther King, Jr, and Senator Robert Kennedy). I would surely add my good friend "Diana" for the woman who discovered land mine use and went public against it. In her documentaries it is often noted, within weeks of her saying we, as humans, need to stop mine use, she too died a disputed death. The Peoples proclaimed Queen of Hearts. Gone for caring for others????

A song of the broken hearts and broken dreams as Abraham Lincoln, John Kennedy, Bob Kennedy and Martin Luther King, Jr. all died in assassinations that even today are still disputed as to how and why they happened. This song relates to the "Straddling the Razor Wire" theme of this book on racism, classism, and hate supported by the system itself.

The disputes, theories and concepts behind the deaths of these people remind us that one person matters, and that some do amazing things, and get killed for it, if some of the theories are to be believed. It is worth the time to study history, and beliefs on each and see what YOU think.

The shocking part of all these deaths is that they occurred in a world in which trust was so broken no one could actually say others were not to be believed. In criminal cases, a crime must be proven (at least in America, under the Constitution, beyond a "reasonable" doubt. None of these deaths could, with all the dispute of the many theories be proven beyond that 'reasonable' doubt. In a regular trial, all the defense lawyers have to do is present a theory that "might" "reasonably" be believed by the jury. How often have we seen cases in which juries gave a mistrial vote because they could not agree on what the evidence given proved, or did not prove.

It seems that in all the doubt and controversy in these deaths, there is NO substantial story with enough support to not be considered to have "reasonable" doubts against all the theories. It is why the American Founders said NO secret government. They wanted "it" all on the table and justice and equality for everyone. If we have secret systems in place that bring doubt to the systems, we must change that. In the Bourne series, both movies but particularly the books, the reality is raised the secret agents are NOT for the law, but working against the law. In interviews the author, a past agent, says, it's not for love of country, the agents are bad guys (and gals). If we break our own principles to get something, as many an active duty, and veteran has raised the issue, what is the point??? Each of us must ask ourselves this question and take part in keeping laws legal for all.

In the Bourne series, books and movies, the author, a retired secret agent poses that these agents are NOT smooth, all for principle, and law James Bonds, who of course breaks laws in such a smooth way we love him. When one person is at risk of a system doing illegal things to them, we ALL at that same risk. We laugh and act like foolish kids in cliques when a person not in "our" gang is illegally destroyed in their job, career, family and reputation in the world, yet when that same treatment comes to us, or someone we "believe" in we are incensed.

Each of us has a duty to read real American history. To look at it, with a questioning eye and mind, and look further if we feel it is needed. The model of America is that we have ONE city, a Federal seat. Those who now want it to be a State are NOT concerned about the NEED for a Federal seat, yet one without more power over the States and cities and individuals than any other. WHY, ask the Natives and farmers in the Northern parts of our country does ANOTHER country get to decide to build pipelines that could, and in fact have, fractured and leaked oil into the water tables and water used for agriculture in those Native Nations and by farmers in those affected States. Who is eating the food and stock fed on that polluted grass and drinking that polluted water from those pipeline leaks??? How many of our veterans are given jobs on those pipeline jobs, and sold quick me up development homes without being told the jobs are for a couple years at most, and they will end up foreclosed out of the homes they bought with their GI loans, and their saved combat pay????? Do we care about our heroes enough to even ask?

WOODIE GUTHRIE, along with Peter, Paul and Mary, and many others sang the song "THIS LAND IS YOUR LAND, THIS LAND IS MY LAND….it IS OUR land, not just the land of a few investors, especially foreign investors and hidden hedge fund investors.

Each of us has a duty to know the history, the hard work done to bring equality to be equal. Each of us has a duty to learn and uphold the principles and laws of the Constitution. The laws and needs of our own State, county, city, family and self! It is what has held America together and put it back together over 200 years of hard learning what it means to live equally and with justice for ALL.

We honestly are floundering in deep quick sand at this moment in history. WE need ALL of us, Anyone on American land or water, or airways NEEDS to get busy, learn the goals, the visions, the principles and make them work without letting violence or any other power shred this first ever human dream of equality and justice for ALL.

BOB DYLAN wrote, Joan Baez, Peter, Paul and Mary, and others sang the song BLOWING IN THE WIND

In the huge not created "BE INs" that happened in San Francisco, Griffith Park, on the beaches and in many other states in support of an end to the Vietnam War, an end to a draft that was not even for a war, certainly not for a war that in any way threatened America itself, and in support of Civil Rights, Women's Rights and Rights for Native Nations and people who even after Civil Rights were legally considered "animals". May Day 1967 across the nation MILLIONS marched for these causes. Along with We Will Overcome, Amazing Grace, and Buffy Saint Marie's UNIVERSAL SOLDIER, BLOWING IN THE WIND was sung in unison without any leadership across these lands.

How many times will a man turn his head

and pretend that he just doesn't see

The answer my friend, is blowing in the wind

The answer is blowing in the wind.

-BOB DYLAN

He's a Catholic, a Hindu, an Atheist, a Jane

A Buddhist, a Baptist and a Jew

He knows he shouldn't kill,

But knows he always will,

Killing for me for friend and me for you

The Universal Soldier, he really is to blame

-BUFFY SAINT MARIE

Amazing Grace, how sweet the sound

That saved a wretch like me

I once was lost, but now am found

Was Blind, but now I see.

JOHN NEWTON(1700's)

Amazing grace has a long and interesting history. Most Baby Boomers remember it from the Civil Rights and End the Draft movements in America of the sixties and seventies.

It was written by a British cleric, John Newton, who was himself forcibly recruited into the Royal Navy and in time became a Captain of his own shipping company and a slaver. It is alleged that he was on a journey from Africa to America to deliver slaves when a huge storm broke at sea......he woke up an abolitionist and wrote the song Amazing Grace as he returned a ship filled with captured Africans to their home country and set them free. The longer history of the song, and. how it became such a standard for the civil rights movements and end the war movements is available on Google.

Ice Cream Man, Round Toed Rubber Soled Shoes

People give me songs. Most couples give their relationship a song, and each other songs. Friends and family often told me songs were for me.

I gave myself Jan and Dean's Little Old Lady of Pasadena. I thought, when I am old, I am going to be a cool little old lady. Play rock and roll while I vacuum, have a cool job, had no idea it would be equine therapy and asking kids to live the life I had so broken by deadly corporate products, drunk drivers, and cancer. Share and enjoy the life they did not want with me for just one year! Not one has ever committed suicide at the end of that loaned year! They find it to have been a great investment in themselves to have followed me around and learned a purpose and take responsibility for their own lives in a positive way.

Crank up Little Old Lady, get in my wheelchair, walk in my crutches, sometimes even braces and get that vacuuming done, wash the dogs, answer the crisis calls and emails to try and help someone enjoy just one hour, a day, a year, and maybe by then so used to happiness and moving towards their dream they do NOT kill themselves.

My sons gave me the commercial background to a perfume ad that said "she can bring home the bacon, cook it up in the pan"…and then they would laugh, knowing they were not supposed to know about the next part "and never let you forget you're a man". They liked commercials at that age, they also gave me the Timex that never stops ticking commercial hum, and the EverReady Bunny. I had realized I would never be able to support them on my salary and had to return to school and a profession after our divorce. I worked one job to care for the house and my sons, another to pay for tuition and costs of returning to school, as well as doing photography, from weddings, to kids, to pets, to Women's Golf, my friend was a woman golfer and said women did not like men photographers in the locker rooms. My sons said, she never stops. Not accidents, eye surgery, divorce. Just kept going.

When I had passed the the first section of the California Bar Exam in 20 minutes, it was a three hour exam, I went home and tried a sample in the mail. It took me eight. years to learn to walk and talk well enough to hold hot horses for my younger son who was becoming a trainer, and had to take me to work because I wandered off and got lost if left at home. Who knew I would keep going and train horses, and start an equine therapy program for high risk kids, and later veterans and first responders and their families. Read my book "Carousel Horse" for the novel and movie script on that portion of my life. Along with working for and getting my Master's Degree for a Racial Tension and Gang Abatement project I had started working WITH, not against the gangs in Los Angeles and Oakland. (This book is to be published next year, MS LIZ, THE LEADER OF THE GANG.

I learned to type and read and write by helping single parent Mothers, often foreign war brides brought home and dumped, speaking many different language to learn how to speak American, and get educations to get jobs and support their children and themselves. Friends helped me put together programs to utilize each of THEIR skills to help these young women and their children. (We have workbooks for single parents to help them make it).

SO, no stopping me.

My friends told me that I "owed" it to women to sue the corporation that had mailed out those samples, I was told by doctors I was going to die, I had seizures from the high fevers, and heart and other organ problems from the enzyme damage of the staph infection that was part of that lovely experience. No one told me then, I found out later while trying to figure out what had happened to me. (One of my lawyers finally won, instead of settling a case and wrote The Price of a Life, by Tom Riley….about a company that cared so little for its consumers it mailed out ten million samples of a product they had been sued for deaths in the test marketing but did not put one sentence in the samples to warn it could KILL you within 45 minutes). And another spike with extra electric pulses was added to that razor coil fence. I did not want to become the fuck you poster child for big corporations, but that's what happened.

When I bought my big four wheelers, i had to change the vision of Little Old Lady of Pasadena, and started a four wheel club for all the women that got tired of getting left home, or left at the RV on big off-road clean-ups of deserts, mountains, rivers beaches and racing events. My sons finally got "Little Old Lady of Pasadena".

If you watch the series Frontmen, on REELZ, David Lee Roth, you will see that Dave was my friend. You will see that with a pending "get on the train, going across country to visit my younger son, and take a picture of all three of us for the first time in 18 years, I did not have time for getting my hair dyed, or shaped, and did not bring a good color of shirt to Pat's house, so had to wear an old garden shirt! Found out my heart medication was not at the pharmacy, so had to go to the doctor and get a new prescription before the deadline for the interview, so no make up, no earrings, just me. It was fun. To do the interview, and to go back and remember those old times when Van Halen practiced in my garage. As noted in my book "Could This Be Magic, a very short book" if. you want to have famous friends, believe in them and help them to build their wings!

Dave used to sing many old Black honky tonk, or whorehouse songs he had learned while learning to play different kinds of music on guitar. We both played regular California music student kid guitar, I had also taken 12 String steel, and classical guitar lessons from college students who also played professionally in bands and classical guitar groups.

He taught me old whorehouse slide.......I still have the slide he gave me somewhere. He used to sing "ICE CREAM MAN" (originally written by John Brim) for our birthday parties, my sons always remember him practicing for open mic nights either at his Dad's big San Marino house, or in our kitchen or patio. He used to sing, either to my sisters, or me, "Dave's got something for you, Liz (or Eva, or Linda)" in that part of the song, we told him sing every song to us, to get the habit of engaging with the audience. First us, then the strangers. He wrote the cutest song, it was similar to the style of "Ice Cream Man" and called "Round Toed Rubber Soled Shoes" I wanted to use it for a movie I had written......but he could not find it. It was about getting up (In spirit) and skipping down the street again!

In the screenplay I wrote about a little Native girl, bussed in off the Rez during the fifties "land steal deals" (the Native Americans called them that) and she hates the city ghetto her family is dumped in, and sees so many Native killed by gangs and people who do not want them there, her father included. Then she sees a poster about a free dance class and gets excited and skips and dances her way home. I thought that song exactly gave the joy of that little girl finally finding something good in a city that did not understand or want all those Natives dumped there by those who wanted their lands now that uranium and oil had been discovered there.

Just Songs

When I was little my Dad used to sing "How much is that doggie in the window", among many other songs of the times, the war, and the fifties. My Mom had been a choir mistress at our huge Episcopal church, and in high school. and college played piano and sang. She was a Girl Scout leader in schools where she taught to help the foster girls, so again was always. singing this or that. She had hundreds of albums of every kind to help her with her work.

She and my Dad were truthfully romantic and danced at home, and even in the street at fairs, etc. My Dad spent years having more than 40 surgeries and was often leg, or body casts and on crutches, but still danced in the streets from time to time just from joy. Mom sang opera and operettas as well as Broadway and musical songs. Christmas songs.

She used to say that little ditty to us from time to time "there was a little girl, had a little curl, right in the middle of her forehead, and when. she was good, she. was very very good, but when she was bad............she. was horrid". Apparently my Grandmother had been fond of the little ditty as well. My Mom had straight blond blond hair as a child, I had curly Native California hair WITH that stupid curl, right in the middle of my forehead when my hair was washed and curled for church or an event. Otherwise my hair, like my sister Eva's,was pulled as tight as possible, parted in the middle and braided on each side of our head for school. For ballet class we had our hair pulled as tight as possible and in that tight bun at the nape of our neck so well known to ballet students. I often wondered why, eyes (and the eyes of the other dancers) did not pop out from that tightly pulled back hair. My Mom was kind enough that at least we did not have a constant look of wide eyed surprise from our hair being pulled back so tight.

At camps, in the big evening campfires each night, one of the songs sung was "when we learn to live serenely.....peace peace peace". Peace I ask of you......oh river, peace, peace, peace. I liked that song because it reminded me of Native American relationships to nature, and the huge river that once passed through our Nation before the Genocide of the Native Californians and the river was stuck into a concrete conduit to give water to big cities rather than the marshlands and wild rice areas of thousands of years for both migrating birds, and humans.

I loved Simon and Garfunkle, 59Th Bridge Song. Since I played guitar from age 12 or 13 and sang, it was a song to sing at campfires and on street corners or parks with the big BE INS and. LOVE INS of the sixties. . After my bout with TSS, I could no longer play the guitar, piano, or remember words to songs. I learned a bit of each over the intervening 42 years.

Writing And Other Thoughts

Put things in order, say lineal people. Manage the grammar and spelling under OUR, the elite rulers, APA rules. Life is not in order.

A "best seller" is the most advertised book. What is a real best seller???? Christmas Carol. Written, it is alleged about the author himself, and challenging each of us to be the Ebenezer of our own lives and yet forgive, change, and be our best and care for each other. Winnie the

Pooh (written by a veteran that today we know suffered from PTSD). Alice in Wonderland, Through the Looking Glass, political commentaries of a time disguised as children's books. Black Beauty, another "children's story" read it again, it's about human beings. Poor Ginger, beaten down and killed by a system she tried to fight and for good reason did not trust…. Beauty, kindly, caring, finally being helped by a little child and the Dad after years of disgusting abuse by the great they and those who gave up caring. THIS book is about humans. Maybe, probably???, one of the reasons I often work with the "Gingers" of this world to facilitate their change of limiting beliefs to live happier, more successful lives.

Books are written for a small elite group who like to subscribe to "best seller" companies, not for the best interest of humanity, or even the authors. William Goldman, author of many books, but most noted, "THE PRINCESS BRIDE" said at one point he had been ordered by the publishers to add another gratuitous sex scene. Instead he wrote, I think those of you who like sex, would rather have it, than read about some made up person having made up sex, but, if you want the pages, write me and I will send them to you. I was learning to write and type again after severe brain injury from high fever staph and wrote. My friend had lent me the book, she being on the mailing list of those who received "best sellers". He wrote back and said, OH, I did not really write one, I am sending another book, hope you enjoy it. THAT book should have been on any best seller book, as well as mandatory for anyone who works with children. WIGGER. A great book. Wish it was still in print. God bless. RIP Mr. Goldman.

At one time we, Americans had said, we need to work hard on making the visions of people such a Thomas Paine, Ben Franklin, George Washington and many others saw of humans finally creating a government OF the PEOPLE, BY the PEOPLE and FOR the people. A recent Stanford history department study was made into a documentary about Ben Franklin's living with and studying Native Nations and how more than 800 nations had lived in peace with care and harmony with Nature and leaving the world better for the next seven generations worked for centuries before a genocidal nightmare with newly invented guns was thrown upon them by the Church, and self appointed monarchs as well as merchants who traded free travel to the new lands in exchange for 50% of everything they ever made or sold as well as the land it was on. No thought for the millions who lived there in peace and harmony with one another and nature for centuries. No thought for the children and young men the great "they" bought from debtor's prisons where their parents bills had left them, or even worse, their parents had sold them to pay the bills and go off to start over, running up new bills.

History NEEDS to be studied, it is not the "aren't we great" pablum sold to school kids and on holidays.

Jefferson and others saw small cities and agricultural areas where all the people were free, no mention of killing off the Natives of three continents to greed it all for a few investors. Jefferson is alleged to have had a slave "wife" after his wife died. Had children with his new wife, who ran his household. Upon his death he freed her, his children and all the slaves from his property. Debtors and banks, as well as old taxes claimed he had no right to dispose of salable property, rounded up all they could catch and sold them. at auction to pay the taxes and bills.

These people saw Washington DC as a NON-state, NON partisan place to meet, once every two years or so, with all the state representatives and senators, and a home for the one short term elected leader, Congress short term elected, and Supreme Court, educated persons who knew the CONSTITUTION, their sole job to rule on questions brought before them, by citizens, by courts, by Congress about the Constitutional reality on any "government" supported legislation or action, national libraries, memorials, and archives, NOT a place that under its treaties must be returned to the States that gave the land for the Capitol of the United States because stupid party politicians got the rabble all "het" up that they deserved another State to give themselves more seats in what is a parliament, no longer a Congress.

Anyone who WORKS in Washington DC is SUPPOSED to be assigned a Congressional District and Senator from their home state. THEY are represented. The party just wants more seats to fight about!

Now "the great they" want to rewrite the Constitution under APA rules. And to fit into a system that is more and more a parliament run by outside lobbyists than short term elected representatives of the electing constituents.

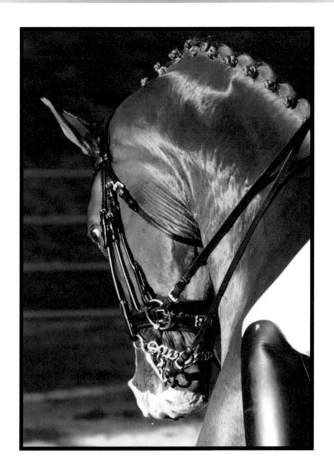

Elton John, Don Mcclean, Dylan

all have to do with those veterans and their active duty brothers in arms saying "what the fuck are we doing here, agent orange destroying rice fields, and wild lands, and murdering children, old men, women and stock animals. Agent Orange that we soon found out was harming our own troops for life.

One special ops Green Beret said he could not get out of his mind, his whole assignment had been to go up and down Vietnam, Laos, and Cambodia using explosives to turn Temples, schools, museums to rubble. He had become a Hell's Angel after his release from the VA hospital, recruited by a group of injured Marines already members of the big biker organization. That organization was NOT a criminal organization, it was a lot of bikers, large numbers of them ex-military who had been injured in body, mind and soul in the NOT wars in Southeast Asia. Large numbers who could not get jobs. They started up their own outside businesses, drugs and arms to the highest bidders. In one summer, Haight /Ashbury and the generation of love turned into the hippy dippie generation and drug addicts. The drugs were being brought home by veterans who could not get treatment for their diseased souls, hearts and minds from the VA, so turned to drugs they had learned to use to manage to survive a war they did not want to be participating in, in countries that did not want them there. Sitting on that electrified razor wire of the draft, and wars they did not want to be in, or being called "commies" by people NOT going to war, who gladly sent those who avoided the draft to prison.

From top bands and solo performers singing free at the parks and beaches, on college campus quads, the streets and alleys became drug, gun and prostitute hangouts. LSD came along and many lost their lives. The top bands, and solo performers died like pathetic flies in fly catchers at the stable, overdosed on illegal street drugs.

One young college student became a recluse, living in an apartment he never left. People brought him meals, and left them outside the door, he watched, waited and grabbed them when he felt safe, He was an acid statistic. He had taken acid and thought he turned into an orange. He thought if any human skin. touched him he would run out. of juice and die. There was NOTHING fun or glamorous in that in my opinion. Look up the history of LSD. Researchers and college students made their own and sold it and gave or sold it for research projects.

"One Pill makes. you larger, the other makes you small"

"The ones that Mother gives you, don't do anything at all"

From the WHITE RABBIT, a very popular song of the late sixties. Grace Slick /Jefferson Airplane.

LSD and drugs became the only savior of soldiers in the S. East Asian not- wars.

Strange, or maybe karma, the Asians prayed for God to bring the "curse of the white powder" on America for what our country did to all of theirs. I think of it every time I hear or read news articles about cocaine, fentynal, heroin. The richest, most powerful to the lowest homeless suffer from these drugs and many forms of meth made in garages and shacks. Their families, neighbors and community members suffer because of the crimes they commit and the harm and often death the addicts cause to themselves. Yet the media continued to portray it as a trendy game, instead of a deadly coping attempt by our soldiers and those they brought the addictions home to.

"Remember what the Door mouse said".

Jefferson Airplane, White Rabbit

Society continues the myth of drugs, rock and roll and flowers in your hair. Jerry Rubin and Abbie Hoffman continue to be portrayed as dippy LSD ruined anti-American traitors. In fact they were college educated men who had to stay in college, and keep their grades up to avoid the draft. They were arrested for passing out subversive material. There was not one world on the page they passed out except a copy of the Constitution. Tells you for one thing that police and District Attorneys had NOT even read the Constitution they each and every one had taken an oath to protect.

AND the other myth of naive, fairytale brain fools America, both Franklin and Jefferson warned us was going to take "constant vigilance" to stay free and equal. We have NOT done that.

Not a positive image to deal with for peace in yourself, in your family, relationships, and block, city, school, community facilities, county, state, nation (all 197 at present of them) and world. (One of our new workshops is the book, " America CAN Live Happily Ever After COVID) To balance harmony with nature before we find out that nature can and will exist without us, but we humans cannot exist without nature.

Peace. In many forms is dealt with in many other workbooks and our hands on, in group programs, such as the equine and animal assisted projects, as well as hands on science to get parents involved in building great science programs for each level of students anywhere in the world. NATURE, all scientists agree, even the most chemical oriented of their crew, is the basis of the chemicals, water, gasses, solids, plants we need to flourish and rebuild and restore this planet we call home.

Closing: Falling on the Razor Wire.

AND MOST IMPORTANTLY, how to take the electrified razor wire down, forever!

Somewhere, no one seems to have an academic research based proof of where, we all begin. There are theories and rumors. Many seem to point to what today is Africa. DNA is showing similarities in most, if not all DNA chains that appear on early theory to say we ALL came from a small area and small group at one time in history and spread over millennia across the planet. .

Beginning a biracial life in 1949 was the falling onto the razor wire for my life. My sister, brother and our half sisters and brothers would all fall on that spiked rolled wire as they came along. Being part Native American, we found is like being part pregnant. The way out is not clear, or easy.

Racism, I would learn 45 years later, in a Masters program in Bicultural Development, is NOT people calling you names, or saying they don't like your culture, religion nation, color of skin. Racism is when the societal organization and systems support that rude name calling and discrimination with a blind eye, or active participation in the harm of the race injured. Racism is genocide. Racism is not about the color of skin. Irish wars of Independence were fought for centuries to repel other white people. Many other wars of Independence we found in research were of many skin colors in home lands. Often white fighting white for freedom. Many of the wars today are one race killing, starving and making slaves out of their own race, culture, even religion shouting and snarling that their form of that religion is THE ONE and GOD IS ON THEIR SIDE to harm anyone not believing THEIR way. Even companies and corporations as surely governments have these conflicts.

FOR GOD'S SAKE in schools, KIDS bully, have gangs, and kill each other.

Racism itself is the POWER to harm, not the hate, or mean spirit of discrimination. When we say "hate crimes" are we giving power to hate, discrimination, prejudice? Is that the opposite of the intention to add years of punishment to racist crimes? When crimes of employment, education, political discrimination, ARE crimes we will begin to free ourselves as humans from racism (classism and financial elitism, which many. countries support by strangely imposed ideas of "education" and money. When a person (many persons) are found to be getting their "education" and passing examinations by paying poverty level technical savvy students in other countries, it is a sham).

When crimes of assault(including maim, manslaughter, even negligent manslaughter, and by vehicle) murder, arson, larceny, and burglary are crimes every single person pays the same for, we will begin to end racism. We are free to dislike anyone we want to, but at least in America, we are NOT free to harm others because of a government sustained self righteousness. The Nazi soldiers hating others did not harm them, its was the illegal actions taken that harmed and murdered others. AND the most important truth of racism, or any other ism is the silence, and complicity of others.

The NAZIs are a horrifying example of what war is, and has been for millennia. At least back two the pharaoh that Moses helped the slaves escape soldiers (doing their job) has been the cause of slavery, anger, and conflict. Those who were "JUST DOING MY JOB". did not stop when they worked for corporations with death dealing products, or toxic waste realities, or cities that allowed corruption and bad practices to go on unstopped harming nature, the environment and people.

The FEW who stood up and said no more to slavery, NO to genocides, and the MANY who finally stood with them are what ends these world crimes of humans were often harmed financially, physically, or even killed, RARELY by those who benefited the most from the crimes against humanity and the earth itself, or animals and nature. They sat at home, receiving regular notices of how "courageous" and "victorious" they were. In the book "A Knight's Tale" by Chaucer, and the movie of the same name, we saw and heard about the racist, classist and narcissistic demands of bad leaders harmed the world.

In the words of the young character alleged to have been based on the young. Chaucer himself, he describes a fat old knight, who because he had "his pattens" was elite, while the young man, hiding behind the armor of his dead knight benefactor to get enough money to feed himself and his friends. The words? "HE sits at banquet, while his countrymen starve to pay the taxes he leavens to pay. For him to be here".

Chaucer was right about saying to the ones who beat him for debts owed that he would "eviscerate them in his words" meaning. in his books. No one remembers ANY of those self aggrandizing people. Only a few of the monarchs left enough material wealth to be "remembered", and few know that even "Good King Wenceslaus" of the Christmas song sung worldwide was a real person. A young man when his father was killed in a war, and he became a teen king. His own mother had been regent and did not want to step down so plotted the death of her own son to get back power.

Yet, thanks to a movie, people today still see the bad people "eviscerated" and the possible hope of a poor Dad to see his son earn, rightly so, honor and money instead of spending his whole life in servitude of a strange human made up system. Based on classism, elitism and as the Bible itself tells us, not even clearly defined ways of how to get to be one of the elite.

King David was a scrawny, small shepherd, his own Father did not think of him as Kingly or one day being powerful. Yet his own belief in God and himself helped him not to just become King, but to attempt to live within the boundaries of God's wishes as he understood them. He failed, he sinned, yet he asked for redemption and grace, and that is how a scrawny shepherd boy became one of the most famous kings of Biblical history.

Late January 1949 I was deposited on this world straddling that electrified razor wire of racism between the Native American and the White Anglo Saxon Protestant (WASP) world.

My Mom said it was a beautiful San Francisco day, the daffodils that had spread wildly across hillsides from old mansion gardens blazing gold on the hillsides behind our home. My Dad, not welcomed in the hospital because of his brown skin, but tolerated because my Mom's wealthy white family was there for their daughter, having taken the train up from Los Angeles. He had not been overly happy to be going to be a Dad, going through many surgeries in the hospital at the Presidio where he had been brought after being found, injured and surviving four years in the wilderness after being shot holding back the Nazi Troops from retreating on D. Day, or from bringing in new supplies to their front lines. Yet, from the street car ride home the morning my Mom and I were released. from hospital, when a stray cigarette butt blew on to my fluffy blanket and set it on fire, even my Mom told everyone my Dad loved me. He put the fire out with his hands, she said, vain as he was, he would have put that fire out with his face to save me, showed how much he loved me.

My parents owned a lovely bow front two story house on Geneva Street. I remember the wood floors, and a small table with a white flower dish, a flower frog (metal spikes sticking up into the air to hold the flowers upright) and the huge cement stair case I fell down before I was two, and the floor heater I fell on, too small to get up fast, and the burns that I still have scars from 70 years later. We sold that house and moved to the Rez when I was four. My Dad and Mom bought a super long Silver Stream trailer for us to live in until my Dad finished building a four bedroom ranch house he had designed and started. That is how our address became "The Silver Trailer by the Creek" on the Dry Creek Rez in Geyserville, California, instead of prestigious Geneva Street in San Francisco.

I remember being two and my sister coming home from the hospital. I loved her from that second on. I remember my brother coming home two years later shortly before we moved north sixty miles to the Rez. I loved him as much as I loved my sister.

From that tasteful and crepe curtain shaded wood floored home, to the same table and floral arrangements in the Silver Trailer squeezed in the narrow living room, I had entered the life of a biracial child not knowing I was straddling that electrified razor wire of not just racism, but classism, and just about any other bias humans could think up, I. seemed to have been born one foot firmly on each side of the razor wire decided abyss of human hatred.

And for the most part, I loved them all.

Our Books And Workbooks:

All of our group of books, and workbooks contain some work pages, and/or suggestions for the reader, and those teaching these books to make notes, to go to computer, and libraries and ask others for information to help these projects work their best.

To utilize these to their fullest, make sure YOU model the increased thoughts and availability of more knowledge to anyone you share these books and workbooks with in classes, or community groups.

Magazines are, as noted in most of the books, a wonderful place to look for and find ongoing research and information. Online search engines often bring up new research in the areas, and newly published material.

We all have examples of how we learned and who it was that taught us.

One of the strangest lessons I have learned was walking to a shoot in downtown Los Angeles. The person who kindly told me to park my truck in Pasadena, and take the train had been unaware that the weekend busses did NOT run early in the morning when the crews had to be in to set up. That person, being just a participant, was going much later in the day, taking a taxi, and had no idea how often crews do NOT carry purses with credit cards, large amounts of cash, and have nowhere to carry those items, because the crew works hard, and fast during a set up and tear down and after the shoot are TIRED and not looking to have to find items that have been left around, or stolen.

As I walked, I had to travel through an area of Los Angeles that had become truly run down and many homeless were encamped about and sleeping on the sidewalks and in alleys. I saw a man, that having worked in an ER for many years I realized was DEAD. I used to have thoughts about people who did not notice people needing help, I thought, this poor man, this is probably the most peace he has had in a long time. I prayed for him and went off to my unwanted walk across town. As I walked, I thought about myself, was I just heartless, or was I truly thinking this was the only moment of peace this man had had for a long time and just leaving him to it. What good were upset neighbors, and police, fire trucks and ambulances going to do. He was calmly, eyes open, staring out at a world that had failed him while alive, why rush to disturb him now that nothing could be done.

I did make sure he was DEAD. He was, quite cold rigid.

I learned that day that it is best to do what a person needs, NOT what we need.

Learning is about introspection and grounding of material. Passing little tests on short term memory skills and not knowing what it all means is NOT education, or teaching.

As a high school student, in accelerated Math and Science programs, in which I received 4.0 grades consistently, I walked across a field, diagonally, and suddenly all that math and science made sense, it was not just exercises on paper I could throw answers back on paper, but I realized had NO clue as to what it all really meant. This meant a lot to me decades later when I was volunteering in a national, then international hands on science education project that offered me aa job to recruit new districts and countries for the FREE preparatory science programs.

Other Books by this Author, and Team

Most, if not all, of these books are written at a fourth grade level. FIrst, the author is severely brain damaged from a high fever disease caused by a sample that came in the mail, without a warning that it had killed during test marketing. After the law suit, when the author recovered enough to wonder what had happened to her, it was discovered that the corporation had known prior to mailing out ten million samples, WITHOUT warnings of disease and known deaths, and then NOT telling anyone after a large number of deaths around the world started.

Second, the target audience is high risk youth, and young veterans, most with a poor education before signing into, or being drafted into the military as a hope Many of our veterans are Vietnam or WWII era.

Maybe those recruiting promises would come true. They would be trained, educated, and given chance for a home, and to protect our country and its principles. Watch the movies Platoon, and Born on the Fourth of July, as well as the Oliver Stone series on history to find out how these dreams were met.

DO NOT bother to write and tell us of grammar or spelling errors. We often wrote these books and workbooks fast for copyrights. We had learned our lessons about giving our material away when one huge charity asked us for our material, promising a grant, Instead, we heard a couple of years later they had built their own VERY similar project, except theirs charged for services, ours were FREE, and theirs was just for a small group, ours was training veterans and others to spread the programs as fast as they could.. They got a Nobel Peace prize. We keep saying we are not bitter, we keep saying we did not do our work to get awards, or thousands of dollars of grants….but, it hurts. Especially when lied to and that group STILL sends people to US for help when they can not meet the needs, or the veterans and family can not afford their "charitable" services. One other group had the nerve to send us a Cease and Desist using our own name. We said go ahead and sue, we have proof of legal use of this name for decades. That man had the conscience to apologize, his program was not even FOR veterans or first responders, or their families, nor high risk kids. But we learned. Sometimes life is very unfair.

We got sued again later for the same issue. We settled out of Court as our programs were just restarting and one of the veterans said, let's just change that part of the name and keep on training veterans to run their own programs. Smart young man.

Book List:

DRAGON KITES and other stories:

The Grandparents Story list will add 12 new titles this year. We encourage every family to write their own historic stories. That strange old Aunt who when you listen to her stories left a rich and well regulated life in the Eastern New York coastal fashionable families to learn Telegraph messaging and go out to the old west to LIVE her life. That old Grandfather or Grandmother who was sent by family in other countries torn by war to pick up those "dollars in the streets" as noted in the book of that title.

Books in publication, or out by summer 2021

Carousel Horse: A Children's book about equine therapy and what schools MIGHT be and are in special private programs.

Carousel Horse: A smaller version of the original Carousel Horse, both contain the workbooks and the screenplays used for on site stable programs as well as lock down programs where the children and teens are not able to go out to the stables.

Spirit Horse II: This is the work book for training veterans and others interested in starting their own Equine Therapy based programs. To be used as primary education sites, or for supplementing public or private school programs. One major goal of this book is to copyright our founding material, as we gave it away freely to those who said they wanted to help us get grants. They did not. Instead they built their own programs, with grant money, and with donations in small, beautiful stables and won….a Nobel Peace Prize for programs we invented. We learned our lessons, although we do not do our work for awards, or grants, we DO not like to be ripped off, so now we copyright.

Reassessing and Restructuring Public Agencies; This book is an over view of our government systems and how they were expected to be utilized for public betterment. This is a Fourth Grade level condemnation of a PhD dissertation that was not accepted be because the mentor thought it was "against government" .. The first paragraph noted that a request had been made, and referrals given by the then White House.

Reassessing and Restructuring Public Agencies; TWO. This book is a suggestive and creative work to give THE PEOPLE the idea of taking back their government and making the money spent and the agencies running SERVE the PEOPLE ;not politicians. This is NOT against government, it is about the DUTY of the PEOPLE to oversee and control government before it overcomes us.

Could This Be Magic? A Very Short Book. This is a very short book of pictures and the author's personal experiences as the Hall of Fame band VAN HALEN practiced in her garage. The pictures are taken by the author, and her then five year old son. People wanted copies of the pictures, and permission was given to publish them to raise money for treatment and long term Veteran homes.

Carousel TWO: Equine therapy for Veterans. publication pending 2021

Carousel THREE: Still Spinning: Special Equine therapy for women veterans and single mothers. This book includes TWELVE STEPS BACK FROM BETRAYAL for soldiers who have been sexually assaulted in the active duty military and help from each other to heal, no matter how horrible the situation. publication pending 2021

LEGAL ETHICS: AN OXYMORON. A book to give to lawyers and judges you feel have not gotten the justice of American Constitution based law (Politicians are great persons to gift with this book). Publication late 2021

PARENTS CAN LIVE and raise great kids.

Included in this book are excerpts from our workbooks from KIDS ANONYMOUS and KIDS JR, and A PARENTS PLAIN RAP (to teach sexuality and relationships to their children. This program came from a copyrighted project thirty years ago, which has been networked into our other programs. This is our training work book. We asked AA what we had to do to become a real Twelve Step program as this is considered a quasi twelve step program children and teens can use to heal BEFORE becoming involved in drugs, sexual addiction, sexual trafficking and relationship woes, as well as unwanted, neglected and abused or having children murdered by parents not able to deal with the reality of parenting. Many of our original students were children of abuse and neglect, no matter how wealthy. Often the neglect was by society itself when children lost parents to illness, accidents or addiction. We were told, send us a copy and make sure you call it quasi. The Teens in the first programs when surveyed for the outcome research reports said, WE NEEDED THIS EARLIER. SO they helped younger children invent KIDS JR. Will be republished in 2021 as a documentary of the work and success of these projects.

Addicted To Dick. This is a quasi Twelve Step program for women in domestic violence programs mandated by Courts due to repeated incidents and danger, or actual injury or death of their children.

Addicted to Dick 2018 This book is a specially requested workbook for women in custody, or out on probation for abuse to their children, either by themselves or their sexual partners or spouses. The estimated national number for children at risk at the time of request was three million across the nation. During Covid it is estimated that number has risen. Homelessness and undocumented families that are unlikely to be reported or found are creating discussion of a much larger number of children maimed or killed in these domestic violence crimes. THE most important point in this book is to force every local school district to train teachers, and all staff to recognize children at risk, and to report their family for HELP, not punishment. The second most important part is to teach every child on American soil to know to ask for help, no matter that parents, or other relatives or known adults, or unknown adults have threatened to kill them for "telling". Most, if not all paramedics, emergency rooms, and police and fire stations are trained to protect the children and teens, and get help for the family.. PUNISHMENT is not the goal, eliminating childhood abuse and injury or death at the hands of family is the goal of all these projects. In some areas JUDGES of child and family courts were taking training and teaching programs themselves to HELP. FREE..

Addicted to Locker Room BS. This book is about MEN who are addicted to the lies told in locker rooms and bars. During volunteer work at just one of several huge juvenile lock downs, where juveniles who have been convicted as adults, but are waiting for their 18th birthday to be sent to adult prisons, we noticed that the young boys and teens had "big" ideas of themselves, learned in locker rooms and back alleys. Hundreds of these young boys would march, monotonously around the enclosures, their lives over. often facing long term adult prison sentences.

The girls, we noticed that the girls, for the most part were smart, had done well in school, then "something" happened. During the years involved in this volunteer work I saw only ONE young girl who was so mentally ill I felt she was not reachable, and should be in a locked down mental health facility for help; if at all possible, and if teachers, and others had been properly trained, helped BEFORE she gotten to that place, lost in the horror and broken of her childhood and early teen years.

We noticed that many of the young women in non military sexual assault healing programs were "betrayed" in many ways, by step fathers, boyfriends, even fathers, and mothers by either molestation by family members, or allowing family members or friends of parents to molest these young women, often as small children. We asked military sexually assaulted young women to begin to volunteer to help in the programs to heal the young girls and teens, it helped heal them all.

There was NOTHING for the boys that even began to reach them until our research began on the locker room BS theory of life destruction and possible salvaging by the boys themselves, and men in prisons who helped put together something they thought they MIGHT have heard before they ended up in prison.

Americans CAN Live Happily Ever After. Parents edition.One

Americans CAN Live Happily Ever After. Children's edition Two.

Americans CAN Live Happily Ever After. Three. After Covid. This book includes "Welcome to America" a requested consult workbook for children and youth finding themselves in cages, auditoriums on cots, or in foster group homes or foster care of relatives or non-relatives with NO guidelines for their particular issues. WE ASKED the kids, and they helped us write this fourth grade level workbook portion of this book to help one another and each other. Written in a hurry! We were asked to use our expertise in other youth programs, and our years of experience teaching and working in high risk youth programs to find something to help.

REZ CHEESE Written by a Native American /WASP mix woman. Using food, and thoughts on not getting THE DIABETES, stories are included of a childhood between two worlds.

REZ CHEESE TWO A continuation of the stress on THE DIABETES needing treatment and health care from birth as well as recipes, and stories from Native America, including thoughts on asking youth to help stop the overwhelming numbers of suicide by our people.

BIG LIZ: LEADER OF THE GANG Stories of unique Racial Tension and Gang Abatement projects created when gangs and racial problems began to make schools unsafe for our children.

DOLLARS IN THE STREETS, ghost edited for author Lydia Caceras, the first woman horse trainer at Belmont Park.

95 YEARS of TEACHING:

A book on teaching, as opposed to kid flipping

Two teachers who have created and implemented systems for private and public education a combined 95 plus years of teaching talk about experiences and realities and how parents can get involved in education for their children. Included are excerpts from our KIDS ANONYMOUS and KIDS JR workbooks of over 30 years of free youth programs.

A HORSE IS NOT A BICYCLE. A book about pet ownership and how to prepare your children for responsible pet ownership and along the way to be responsible parents. NO ONE needs to own a pet, or have a child, but if they make that choice, the animal, or child deserves a solid, caring forever home.

OLD MAN THINGS and MARE'S TALES. this is a fun book about old horse trainers I met along the way. My husband used to call the old man stories "old man things", which are those enchanting and often very effective methods of horse, pet, and even child rearing. I always said I brought up my children and my students the same as I had trained horses and dogs......I meant that horses and dogs had taught me a lot of sensible, humane ways to bring up an individual, caring, and dream realizing adult who was HAPPY and loved.

STOP TALKING, DO IT

ALL of us have dreams, intentions, make promises. This book is a workbook from one of our programs to help a person make their dreams come true, to build their intentions into goals, and realities, and to keep their promises. One story from this book, that inspired the concept is a high school kid, now in his sixties, that was in a special ed program for drug abuse and not doing well in school. When asked, he said his problem was that his parents would not allow him to buy a motorcycle. He admitted that he did not have money to buy one, insure one, take proper driver's education and licensing examinations to own one, even though he had a job. He was asked to figure out how much money he was spending on drugs. Wasting his own money, stealing from his parents and other relatives, and then to figure out, if he saved his own money, did some side jobs for neighbors and family until he was 18, he COULD afford the motorcycle and all it required to legally own one. In fact, he did all, but decided to spend the money on college instead of the motorcycle when he graduated from high school. His priorities had changed as he learned about responsible motorcycle ownership and risk doing the assignments needed for his special ed program. He also gave up drugs, since his stated reason was he could not have a motorcycle, and that was no longer true, he COULD have a motorcycle, just had to buy it himself, not just expect his parents to give it to him.

STRADDLING THE RAZOR WIRE.

Straddling The Razor Wire is not about what others do, it is about ALL OF US, together, living OUR own life, in this very moment, happily and together. This is a trilogy of books, RAZOR WIRE I, II, III.

STRADDLING THE RAZOR WIRE II

A TRILOGY of our Equine Therapy work.

This book is a trilogy of. our work with veterans and high risk youth, each one with a script.

RAZOR WIRE III: STRADDLING AGAIN:

REASSESSING AND RESTRUCTURING PUBLIC AGENCIES II is what the third of the trilogy is about. It is about wanting to be a good American, but having to deal with the realities that something is very wrong and the DUTY of every person on American soil to be part of fixing itt.

SITTING RIGHT ON TOP OF THE RAZOR WIRE is how I feel about even saying anything about what is wrong with our country. Recently a friend in Virginia received a letter from their Congressperson apologizing for not running again, explaining that the corrupt and dirty politics was just to0 much to put his family through.

It reminded me of a scene in "Legally Blonde II" in which a Congresswoman says she. has to be corrupt or she will not be re-elected and then can do NOTHING. The young lawyer tells her, you are NOT doing anyone any good supporting that thought.

A young person, challenged by friends to run for that seat said she honestly did not want to put her family into such a nightmare in case one of THEM might have done something to get grabbed by the gossip press and spread around. What on earth does its have to do with anything what your relations are up to. If it really meant anything a leading family from at least one country should be kicked out the antics of one of their family members.

Applying the Constitution, Declaration of Independence, United Nations Constitution AND using the most complex public agencies book in the world (THE MANUAL OF THE UNITED STATES GOVERNMENT) suggesting to developed, and developing nations how to structure public agency infrastructure as well as oversight to keep the voters, and taxpayers aware of their rights and how to demand proper management of their assets and agencies for public service, not public torment and harassment.

During these horrifying years of natural disasters, war, crime some humans, even some leaders have come out of the disasters and not waited, not had panel discussions, not gone to "view" the damage. Instead, as amazing journalists and photographers have shown us, and a few leaders have awarded, people have gotten others to join together and resolve the problems by their heartfelt service to our Creator, no matter what their religion, or stated anti-religion, they have served, both God and humans. Many have returned to protect, and open other eyes, and are restoring nature. What is the excuse of others???

Explanation of Additional Books

Explanation:

Our books are written as on ongoing series for high risk youth, veterans, and first responders as well as their parents and those who are raising them.

One of the reasons for starting this series was we, as special needs teachers, as therapists, as Directors of programs and private schools for high risk youth began to recognize how many of the children and youth were children of veterans, grandchildren of veterans, and also first responders. This included police, fire, paramedic and nurses and doctors in first response or frontline positions in intensive care work.

We then noticed the numbers of minority children and poverty level financial back grounds were the reality for high risk children and youth. We saw children of Mothers who had been as young as NINE at the birth of their child among the high risk students. Whether rich, or poverty level, we saw children born to parents who suffered suffered alcohol, sexual, gambling and drug addictions among many other addictions. Compulsive cleaning, exercising, shopping, gossiping, dieting and hoarding of things, pets, as well as bad relationships are among but a few.

We saw children as young as 18 months labeled with an alphabet of mental health disorders, medicated and put into "special schools" where in fact found by media just victims of scamming on social service taxpayer dollars. The children and teens were often warehoused, abused, and not taught at all. Upon seeing a news story about the schools discovered at some of the licensed sites, in which children and teens often did not have desks, or chairs to sit on, let alone proper educational supplies and equipment for special learning program, we joined with others, and designed programs.

We were naive enough to think our work, offered FREE in most cases, would be welcomed especially as we offer it free and often through research projects, but, it was NOT valued or wanted.

What? we asked?

We went back to college and while earning degrees we had apparently NOT needed while working with children of the very rich in expensive private schools, we did research projects to document our findings. To find ways to overcome the problems. Again, our work was NOT valued or wanted.

One of our associates, who had asked many of us to volunteer in a once a month FREE reading program in the local public schools, was held back for almost two years doing paperwork and proving her volunteers, most of them parents of successful children, teens and adults, could read a first five years book and teach parents how to read those books to their own children. She was a Deputy United States Prosecutor, and had recruited friends from all levels of law enforcement, child and family services, education and volunteer groups that served children and families.

Currently the truth is coming out, of many parents who thought they had enough money to over ride ethics, morality and even the justice system being convicted (many others pled guilty) of corruption in getting their children enrolled on sports scholarship to colleges and graduate programs they were not qualified to attend. We all wonder, what about those who "went" to college and graduate school by paying other students or professional students doing the work for them, as is currently being revealed. Great to find out your doctor, dentist, lawyer is NOT qualified to do the job, some foreign professional student did the learning!

None the less, we continued our work, met a fabulous and expensive Psychiatrist who was building his own server system and the first online education project after creating a massive and encompassing medical examination study guide for graduate medical students to assist them in passing global and national medical examinations for licensing.

We worked with a team of citizens and specialists in education who had created a 39 manual project for students, parents and teachers to be able to learn on their own.

This series of books includes ideas, history and thoughts from the students, the parents, and professionals who work with these situations.

Jesus was told, don't have children wasting your time, and he responded, let the children come.

Our work is to bring children to us, and to those who have the heart and love to develop the uniqueness and individuality of each of God's creations. Many of them are of different religions, and beliefs, and many are atheists but believe fully in the wonder and uniqueness of every human.

To all who have helped and continue to help children and anyone wanting to learn, we thank God and we thank you.

Closing:Closing and Other Books by Author and team

Closing Straddling The Razor Wire is not about what others do, it is about ALL OF US, together, living OUR own life, in this very moment, happily and together.

Closing:

All of our group of books, and workbooks contain some work pages, and/or suggestions for the reader, and those teaching these books to make notes, to go to computer, and libraries and ask others for information to help these projects work their best.

To utilize these to their fullest, make sure YOU model the increased thoughts and availability of more knowledge to anyone you share these books and workbooks with in classes, or community groups.

Magazines are, as noted in most of the books, a wonderful place to look for and find ongoing research and information. Online search engines often bring up new research in the areas, and newly published material.

We all have examples of how we learned and who it was that taught us.

One of the strangest lessons I have learned was walking to a shoot in downtown Los Angeles. The person who kindly told me to park my truck in Pasadena, and take the train had been unaware that the weekend busses did NOT run early in the morning when the crews had to be in to set up. That person, being just a participant, was going much later in the day, taking a taxi, and had no idea how often crews do NOT carry purses with credit cards, large amounts of cash, and have nowhere to carry those items, because the crew works hard, and fast during a set up and tear down and after the shoot are TIRED and not looking to have to find items that have been left around, or stolen.

As I walked, I had to travel through an area of Los Angeles that had become truly run down and many homeless were encamped about and sleeping on the sidewalks and in alleys. I saw a man, that having worked in an ER for many years I realized was DEAD. I used to have thoughts about people who did not notice people needing help, I thought, this poor man, this is probably the most peace he has had in a long time. I prayed for him and went off to my unwanted walk across town. As I walked, I thought about myself, was I just heartless, or was I truly thinking this was the only moment of peace this man had had for a long time and just leaving him to it. What good were upset neighbors, and police, fire trucks and ambulances going to do. He was calmly, eyes open, staring out at a world that had failed him while alive, why rush to disturb him now that nothing could be done.

I did make sure he was DEAD. He was, quite cold rigid.

I learned that day that it is best to do what a person needs, NOT what we need.

Learning is about introspection and grounding of material. Passing little tests on short term memory skills and not knowing what it all means is NOT education, or teaching.

As a high school student, in accelerated Math and Science programs, in which I received 4.0 grades consistently, I walked across a field, diagonally, and suddenly all that math and science made sense, it was not just exercises on paper I could throw answers back on paper, but I realized had NO clue as to what it all really meant. This meant a lot to me decades later when I was volunteering in a national, then international hands on science education project that offered me aa job to recruit new districts and countries for the FREE preparatory science programs

Additional thoughts and BOOKS by this author, and team

Most, if not all, of these books are written at a fourth grade level. FIrst, the author is severely brain damaged from a high fever disease caused by a sample that came in the mail, without a warning that it had killed during test marketing. During the law suit, it was discovered that the corporation had known prior to mailing out ten million samples, WITHOUT warnings of disease and known deaths, and then NOT telling anyone after a large number of deaths around the world started. Second, the target audience is high risk youth, and young veterans, most with a poor education before signing into, or being drafted into the military as a hope Many of our veterans are Vietnam or WWII era.

Maybe those recruiting promises would come true. They would be trained, educated, and given chance for a home, and to protect our country and its principles. Watch the movies Platoon, and Born on the Fourth of July as well as the Oliver Stone series on history to find out how these dreams were meet.

DO NOT bother to write and tell us of grammar or spelling errors. We often wrote these books and workbooks fast for copyrights. We had learned our lessons about giving our material away when one huge charity asked us for our material, promising a grant, Instead, we heard a couple of years later they had built their own VERY similar project, except theirs charged for services, ours were FREE, and theirs was just for a small group, ours was training veterans and others to spread the programs as fast as they could.. They got a Nobel Peace prize. We keep saying we are not bitter, we keep saying we did not do our work to get awards, or thousands of dollars of grants....but, it hurts. Especially when lied to and that group STILL sends people to US for help when they can not meet the needs, or the veterans and family can not afford their "charitable" services. One other group had the nerve to send us a Cease and Desist using our own name. We said go ahead and sue, we have proof of legal use of this name for decades. That man had the conscience to apologize, his program was not even FOR veterans or first responders, or their families, nor high risk kids. But we learned. Sometimes life is very unfair.

We got sued again later for the same issue. We settled out of Court as our programs were just restarting and one of the veterans said, let's just change that part of the name and keep on training veterans to run their own programs. Smart young man.

Book List:

DRAGON KITES and other stories:

The Grandparents Story list will add 12 new titles this year. We encourage every family to write their own historic stories. That strange old Aunt who when you listen to her stories left a rich and well regulated life in the Eastern New York coastal fashionable families to learn Telegraph messaging and go out to the old west to LIVE her life. That old Grandfather or Grandmother who was sent by family in other countries torn by war to pick up those "dollars in the streets" as noted in the book of that title.

Books in publication, or out by summer 2021

Carousel Horse: A Children's book about equine therapy and what schools MIGHT be and are in special private programs.

Carousel Horse: A smaller version of the original Carousel Horse, both contain the workbooks and the screenplays used for on site stable programs as well as lock down programs where the children and teens are not able to go out to the stables.

Spirit Horse II: This is the work book for training veterans and others interested in starting their own Equine Therapy based programs. To be used as primary education sites, or for supplementing public or private school programs. One major goal of this book is to copyright our founding material, as we gave it away freely to those who said they wanted to help us get grants. They did not. Instead they built their own programs, with grant money, and with donations in small, beautiful stables and won....a Nobel Peace Prize for programs we invented. We learned our lessons, although we do not do our work for awards, or grants, we DO not like to be ripped off, so now we copyright.

Reassessing and Restructuring Public Agencies; This book is an over view of our government systems and how they were expected to be utilized for public betterment. This is a Fourth Grade level condemnation of a PhD dissertation that was not accepted be because the mentor thought it was "against government" .. The first paragraph noted that a request had been made, and referrals given by the then White House.

Reassessing and Restructuring Public Agencies; TWO. This book is a suggestive and creative work to give THE PEOPLE the idea of taking back their government and making the money spent and the agencies running SERVE the PEOPLE ;not politicians. This is NOT against government, it is about the DUTY of the PEOPLE to oversee and control government before it overcomes us.

Could This Be Magic? A Very Short Book. This is a very short book of pictures and the author's personal experiences as the Hall of Fame band VAN HALEN practiced in her garage. The pictures are taken by the author, and her then five year old son. People wanted copies of the pictures, and permission was given to publish them to raise money for treatment and long term Veteran homes.

Carousel TWO: Equine therapy for Veterans. publication pending 2021

Carousel THREE: Still Spinning: Special Equine therapy for women veterans and single mothers. This book includes TWELVE STEPS BACK FROM BETRAYAL for soldiers who have been sexually assaulted in the active duty military and help from each other to heal, no matter how horrible the situation. publication pending 2021

LEGAL ETHICS: AN OXYMORON. A book to give to lawyers and judges you feel have not gotten the justice of American Constitution based law (Politicians are great persons to gift with this book). Publication late 2021

PARENTS CAN LIVE and raise great kids.

Included in this book are excerpts from our workbooks from KIDS ANONYMOUS and KIDS JR, and A PARENTS PLAIN RAP (to teach sexuality and relationships to their children. This program came from a copyrighted project thirty years ago, which has been networked into our other programs. This is our training work book. We asked AA what we had to do to become a real Twelve Step program as this is considered a quasi twelve step program children and teens can use to heal BEFORE becoming involved in drugs, sexual addiction, sexual trafficking and relationship woes, as well as unwanted, neglected and abused or having children murdered by parents not able to deal with the reality of parenting. Many of our original students were children of abuse and neglect, no matter how wealthy. Often the neglect was by society itself when children lost parents to illness, accidents or addiction.

We were told, send us a copy and make sure you call it quasi. The Teens in the first programs when surveyed for the outcome research reports said, WE NEEDED THIS EARLIER. SO they helped younger children invent KIDS JR. Will be republished in 2021 as a documentary of the work and success of these projects.

Addicted To Dick. This is a quasi Twelve Step program for women in domestic violence programs mandated by Courts due to repeated incidents and danger, or actual injury or death of their children.

Addicted to Dick 2018 This book is a specially requested workbook for women in custody, or out on probation for abuse to their children, either by themselves or their sexual partners or spouses. The estimated national number for children at risk at the time of request was three million across the nation. During Covid it is estimated that number has risen. Homelessness and undocumented families that are unlikely to be reported or found are creating discussion of a much larger number of children maimed or killed in these domestic violence crimes. THE most important point in this book is to force every local school district to train teachers, and all staff to recognize children at risk, and to report their family for HELP, not punishment. The second most important part is to teach every child on American soil to know to ask for help, no matter that parents, or other relatives or known adults, or unknown adults have threatened to kill them for "telling". Most, if not all paramedics, emergency rooms, and police and fire stations are trained to protect the children and teens, and get help for the family.. PUNISHMENT is not the goal, eliminating childhood abuse and injury or death at the hands of family is the goal of all these projects. In some areas JUDGES of child and family courts were taking training and teaching programs themselves to HELP. FREE..

Addicted to Locker Room BS. This book is about MEN who are addicted to the lies told in locker rooms and bars. During volunteer work at just one of several huge juvenile lock downs, where juveniles who have been convicted as adults, but are waiting for their 18th birthday to be sent to adult prisons, we noticed that the young boys and teens had "big" ideas of themselves, learned in locker rooms and back alleys. Hundreds of these young boys would march, monotonously around the enclosures, their lives over. often facing long term adult prison sentences.

The girls, we noticed that the girls, for the most part were smart, had done well in school, then "something" happened. During the years involved in this volunteer work I saw only ONE young girl who was so mentally ill I felt she was not reachable, and should be in a locked down mental health facility for help; if at all possible, and if teachers, and others had been properly trained, helped BEFORE she gotten to that place, lost in the horror and broken of her childhood and early teen years.

We noticed that many of the young women in non military sexual assault healing programs were "betrayed" in many ways, by step fathers, boyfriends, even fathers, and mothers by either molestation by family members, or allowing family members or friends of parents to molest these young women, often as small children. We asked military sexually assaulted young women to begin to volunteer to help in the programs to heal the young girls and teens, it helped heal them all.

There was NOTHING for the boys that even began to reach them until our research began on the locker room BS theory of life destruction and possible salvaging by the boys themselves, and men in prisons who helped put together something they thought they MIGHT have heard before they ended up in prison.

Americans CAN Live Happily Ever After. Parents edition.One

Americans CAN Live Happily Ever After. Children's edition Two.

Americans CAN Live Happily Ever After. Three. After Covid. This book includes "Welcome to America" a requested consult workbook for children and youth finding themselves in cages, auditoriums on cots, or in foster group homes or foster care of relatives or non-relatives with NO guidelines for their particular issues. WE ASKED the kids, and they helped us write this fourth grade level workbook portion of this book to help one another and each other. Written in a hurry! We were asked to use our expertise in other youth programs, and our years of experience teaching and working in high risk youth programs to find something to help.

REZ CHEESE Written by a Native American / WASP mix woman. Using food, and thoughts on not getting THE DIABETES, stories are included of a childhood between two worlds.

REZ CHEESE TWO A continuation of the stress on THE DIABETES needing treatment and health care from birth as well as recipes, and stories from Native America, including thoughts on asking youth to help stop the overwhelming numbers of suicide by our people.

BIG LIZ: LEADER OF THE GANG Stories of unique Racial Tension and Gang Abatement projects created when gangs and racial problems began to make schools unsafe for our children.

DOLLARS IN THE STREETS, ghost edited for author Lydia Caceras, the first woman horse trainer at Belmont Park.

95 YEARS of TEACHING:

A book on teaching, as opposed to kid flipping

Two teachers who have created and implemented systems for private and public education a combined 95 plus years of teaching talk about experiences and realities and how parents can get involved in education for their children. Included are excerpts from our KIDS ANONYMOUS and KIDS JR workbooks of over 30 years of free youth programs.

A HORSE IS NOT A BICYCLE. A book about pet ownership and how to prepare your children for responsible pet ownership and along the way to be responsible parents. NO ONE needs to own a pet, or have a child, but if they make that choice, the animal, or child deserves a solid, caring forever home.

OLD MAN THINGS and MARE'S TALES. this is a fun book about old horse trainers I met along the way. My husband used to call the old man stories "old man things", which are those enchanting and often very effective methods of horse, pet, and even child rearing. I always said I brought up my children and my students the same as I had trained horses and dogs......I meant that horses and dogs had taught me a lot of sensible, humane ways to bring up an individual, caring, and dream realizing adult who was HAPPY and loved.

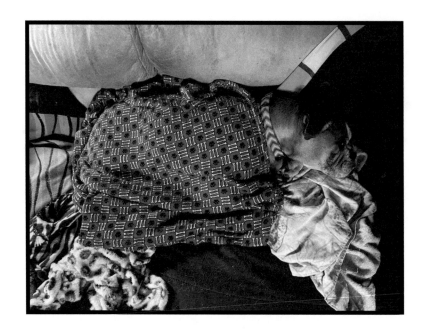

Stop Talking, Do It

ALL of us have dreams, intentions, make promises. This book is a workbook from one of our programs to help a person make their dreams come true, to build their intentions into goals, and realities, and to keep their promises. One story from this book, that inspired the concept is a high school kid, now in his sixties, that was in a special ed program for drug abuse and not doing well in school. When asked, he said his problem was that his parents would not allow him to buy a motorcycle. He admitted that he did not have money to buy one, insure one, take proper driver's education and licensing examinations to own one, even though he had a job. He was asked to figure out how much money he was spending on drugs. Wasting his own money, stealing from his parents and other relatives, and then to figure out, if he saved his own money, did some side jobs for neighbors and family until he was 18, he COULD afford the motorcycle and all it required to legally own one. In fact, he did all, but decided to spend the money on college instead of the motorcycle when he graduated from high school. His priorities had changed as he learned about responsible motorcycle ownership and risk doing the assignments needed for his special ed program. He also gave up drugs, since his stated reason was he could not have a motorcycle, and that was no longer true, he COULD have a motorcycle, just had to buy it himself, not just expect his parents to give it to him.

Printed in the United States
by Baker & Taylor Publisher Services